S TO

GY

ard

Hodder & Stoughton
A MEMBER OF THE HODDER HEADLINE GROUP

Acknowledgements

The publishers would like to thank the following for permission to reproduce photographs and other illustrations in this book:

Page 4 (1.02), Andy Warrington; **p6** (1.04), Andy Warrington; **p8** (1.05), Albert Bandura, Stanford University; **p37** (2.09), © Hans Reinhard/Okapia Oxford Scientific Films; **p38** (2.10), Andy Warrington; **p39** (2.11), Andy Warrington; **p40** (2.12), The Wellcome Library, London; **p43** (2.14) © Paul Franklin/Oxford Scientific Films; **p45** (2.15), Action Plus; **p47** (2.16), Sue Swales; **p48** (2.17) Sue Swales; **p54** (3.01), Professor K. Seddon and Dr. T. Evans, Queen's University Belfast/Science Photo Library; **p56** (3.02), Rex Features Limited/Barbara Herbert/Daphne Goodship; **p59** (3.03), Andy Warrington; **p60** (3.04), Andy Warrington; **p69** (4.01), Bettmann/Corbis; **p72** (4.03), Action Plus; **p76** (4.07), Hulton-Deutsch Collection/Corbis; **p79** (4.09), Megasnaps/Ace; **p82** (4.11), News Of The World; **p88** (4.14), Science Photo Library; **p92** (4.16), Michael Papo/Famous; **p102** (5.01), John Wiley & Sons, Inc.; **p105** (5.02), © Life File/Nicola Sutton; **p106** (5.03), Colorstock/Ace; **p110** (5.04), Action Plus; **p122** (6.01), Austin J. Brown, the Aviation Picture Library; **p126** (6.02), Geoff du Feu/Ace; **p128** (6.03), Schenectady Museum: Hall of Electrical History Foundation/Corbis; **p130** (6.04), PA Photos; **p132** (6.05), Andy Warrington; **p137** (7.01), © William Gray/Oxford Scientific Films; **p140** (7.03), © 1972 by Scientific American Inc. All rights reserved; **p141** (7.04), Ron Sutherland/Science Photo Library; **p144** (7.06), AP Photo/Dennis Redman; **p146** (7.07a), PA Photos; **p146** (7.07b), David and Peter Turnley/Corbis; **p150** (7.09), Oscar Burriel/Science Photo Library; **p153** (7.10), 'Speed: Nature fights back', July 2001 © BBC Picture Archives; **p158** (7.12), Fotopic/Ace; **p164** (8.01), AP Photo/Mike Fisher; **p166** (8.03), Andy Warrington; **p167** (8.04), Raoul Minsart/Corbis; **p170** (8.05), AP Photo/John Gaps III.

Every effort has been made to obtain necessary permission with reference to copyright material. The publishers apologise if inadvertently any sources remain unacknowledged and will be glad to make the necessary arrangements at the earliest opportunity.

Orders; please contact Bookpoint Ltd, 130 Milton Park, Abingdon, Oxon OX14 4SB. Telephone: (44) 01235 827720, Fax: (44) 01235 400454. Lines are open from 9.00–6.00, Monday to Saturday, with a 24 hour message answering service.
Email address: orders@bookpoint.co.uk

British Library Cataloguing in Publication Data
A catalogue record for this title is available from the British Li

ISBN 0 340 80417 3

First published 2001

Impression number   10 9 8 7 6 5 4 3 2 1
Year   2005 2004 2003 2002 2001
Copyright © 2001 Karon Oliver

Typeset by GreenGate Publishing Services, Tonbridge, Kent.

Printed in Great Britain for Hodder and Stoughton Educational, a division of Hodder Headline Plc, 338 Euston Road, London NW1 3BH, by Martins the Printers Ltd, Berwick-upon-Tweed.

Contents

- Surveys/questionnaires/interviews
- Physiological measurements
- Correlations
- Problems with sampling

Problems of data collection and measurement and interpretation
(including reliability and validity)

- Extraneous or confounding variables
- Demand characteristics
- Experimenter effects
- Experimenter bias

The history of ethical guidelines and the current BPS code

- Consent
- Deception
- Debriefing
- Withdrawal
- Privacy
- Protection of participants
- Observations

- Ethnocentrism
- Cultural relativism (and ethics)
- Ecological validity
- Is the research recent?
- Subject variables

- Does old equal 'out of date'?
- Can we apply the research to new situations?
- What are the implications of psychological research?

- Questions asking you to describe
- Questions asking you to evaluate
- Questions asking you to apply

Introduction

We are all amateur psychologists and have opinions and ideas about why people behave the way they do. Consequently, when we learn about psychology, we usually find the subject interesting, enjoyable and relatively easy to understand. In fact, classroom discussions are an important part of learning, because they allow us to test our ideas and exchange views with each other. I am sure that you can all remember class discussions that you have had, and how enlightening they can be, allowing you to see topics from other perspectives.

The trouble is that when it comes to applying our understanding of psychology in an examination, many students find that their ability to argue and think rationally goes out of the window. Part of the problem is knowing how to answer examination questions which require not only factual information but also opinion. Psychology requires very different skills from some other disciplines, as there are often no absolutely right or wrong answers, simply differing points of view, many of which are contradictory, but which must, of course, be backed up by evidence. I remember my first psychology essay – 'Memory is like a tape recorder – discuss'. I knew what I wanted to say, but wondered who would really be interested in my opinion. To try and explain why and how I felt about memory filled me with dread.

Fortunately, many of the A2 Psychology examinations have questions which are less ambiguous, and if you know your stuff, you should have a good idea of what sort of information you ought to be thinking about. However, actually writing that information down, effectively and concisely, doesn't come naturally to many students. Having the confidence to answer questions effectively comes only from understanding what the examiners want, and this, I hope, will be one of the skills you learn from this book.

I have the feeling that if one of my teachers had given me a book which aimed to help me develop the skills I needed when describing, evaluating and applying psychological research, I would have immediately put it down and gone to sleep. Even if I managed to read the first page or so, I expect I would have nodded off soon. I can't guarantee that you will find all of this book stunningly exciting and interesting.

However, I hope that if you manage to stick with it, it will help you to think carefully about the things that you read, and as a result, manage to write good essays and impress your examiner. I have tried to make the topics as user-friendly as I can because all of you will have interesting opinions about what you read, but often you don't write them down in case they are wrong.

This book has been planned to explore the types of questions that students are asked in examinations, especially the OCR A2 syllabus. However, most examination questions require students to show that they not only know about certain studies, but that they also understand them and can evaluate them effectively. Students also need to be aware of the studies' relevance to real life, and not simply as isolated research that has no practical application.

The book first considers *how to describe*, then *ways of evaluating* and finally *how to apply that knowledge* to everyday life. The final chapters address how to put all the topics covered together and write mature, comprehensive essays in a way that should impress your examiners. Four things to remember when constructing an essay:

- Why was a study conducted?
- What were the findings and what did they mean?
- Was the study well designed?
- Could you apply the findings to other issues?

Once you have learned the skills to address these questions, you can use them over and over again, and apply them to all aspects of psychology, whether you are reading for pleasure, for A level or beyond. Now it's your turn to really think about what you read and to sort out your own opinions.

What psychological research means

An overview of the requirements to answer questions about psychology effectively, even if they are questions from your best friend.

- **How to describe ...**
- **What is meant by evaluation?**
- **Comparing and contrasting**

HOW TO DESCRIBE ...

Very few people have difficulty in describing psychological research. If you have a good memory, you can reel off details of past studies with no problems, a bit like a shopping list of research. The trouble is, we can all go away and learn things and then regurgitate them, but it doesn't actually show that you really understand what that information means. I remember a situation where this happened to me. I was trying to impress this particular male by sounding very knowledgeable about all sorts of things. In fact, I was talking about my old school and recited the Latin motto 'Dulce et decorum est pro patria mori'. He was very impressed and thought I was brilliant and could speak Latin. I stupidly didn't tell him that I knew it only because it was on the badge on my blazer and I had to look at it every day. Anyway, he seemed suitably impressed but I became completely unstuck one day when I was asked to translate a piece of Latin text and had to admit that I hadn't a clue. His illusions were shattered and he disappeared into the sunset. I knew the information but I didn't understand it, which made it meaningless.

Hopefully, this story should make you realise that when you describe psychological research, it is really important to understand it. Why did it happen? How can you explain the findings? I remember marking essay after essay and writing 'Why?' in the margin time after time. Students described with total accuracy all sorts of bizarre pieces of research, but omitted to explain what they meant. Even when some of the studies described lacked detail because it was not available to them in the various textbooks they had read, they still needed to know the results and be able to explain them. If you think about it, it's not fair to expect full marks in an examination for something you have simply learned but maybe don't understand. You must also look at how the findings can relate to real life – in a wider context.

Let me give you an example taken from **health psychology**:

> Robinson and West (1992) investigated the amount of information people gave when they attended a genito-urinary clinic (a clinic specialising in sexually transmitted diseases). Before they saw the doctor, patients were asked to give intimate details of their symptoms, to state whether they had attended a genito-urinary clinic before and also to provide information about their sexual behaviour. They were told to give the information either by filling in a questionnaire (one group) or to answer a series of questions on a computer (the other group). The results were that people gave more significant information to the computer than they did to a written questionnaire.

'So what?', you may say. What does this study suggest? Actually, the purpose of the study was to look at the reluctance of patients to disclose their symptoms. The findings suggest that people were unwilling to give the information to a written questionnaire, presumably because the receptionist might see the information whilst they were still in the surgery and make some kind of judgement about them. On the other hand, a computer would be non-judgemental and the data provided would have to be directly accessed in order for anyone to see it. Strictly speaking, the data given to the computer could have potentially been made available to far more people than the receptionist. Therefore we need to accept the possibility that when people are frightened of being judged, they don't necessarily think rationally about what they are doing.

You can see that the box above simply describes the study; I haven't actually *explained* anything very much. I haven't shown that I have any real psychological knowledge but have simply regurgitated what I've been told. My conclusion was just speculation, of course, and one of a number of conclusions that could be drawn.

When you first read this study, perhaps you felt that the results showed that the patients couldn't actually write or loved computers to distraction rather than having a deeper psychological explanation. The speculation may be incorrect, but at least it's based on psychological concepts. After all, the only way that the researchers could have found out whether their speculations were correct would have been by questioning the patients. This may have highlighted ethical issues (did the participants know they were taking part in the study?).

Another example comes from **environmental psychology** where researchers were interested in looking at the effects of heat on aggressive behaviour. They were investigating the **negative affect escape model** which predicts that with rising temperature aggression increases to a certain level. After a point it decreases because the person becomes so uncomfortable that their aggression subsides as they focus attention on escaping from that discomfort.

A study by Baron and Bell (1975) supports this idea that there is an inverted U relationship between arousal and response (and also supports the negative affect escape model). They arranged for subjects to be either insulted or complimented by a stooge and then gave subjects the opportunity to give the stooge electric shocks in different temperatures.

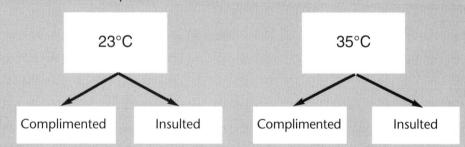

Figure 1.1

As expected, the 23°C subjects gave more shocks to the insulting person than to the complimentary stooge, but in the 35°C condition the opposite occurred. In fact they reduced the shocks given to the insulting stooge and gave more shocks to the complimentary one. This can be explained by the idea that together the insulting stooge and the high temperature raised the arousal level of the subjects over the top of the peak of the inverted U, so they began to feel less aggressive, whereas the complimentary stooge neither increased or decreased their levels of arousal.

The second paragraph in the box gives a possible reason for the participants in this research acting as they did, rather than simply stating the obvious. It is here that psychology students can demonstrate that they really do understand what it's all about rather than just reproducing notes; often there is more than one explanation of the research findings – can you think of any others? Students can also show their understanding that this information can be applied more generally by mentioning that over-arousal can also apply to other types of situations and cause similar results.

Let me give you one final description of some research which is relevant to both **sports** and **environmental psychology**. This research is often described accurately but the reasons for the results are omitted. These examples can be used in either one of these specialist areas, but they would be explained in a slightly different way depending on whether you were looking from the perspective of sports psychology or environmental psychology.

These examples look at something called the 'home court advantage'. The home court advantage is where sports teams seem to do better when they compete on their own territory rather than at 'away' matches. In fact, Altman (1975) found that the University of Utah football team won two-thirds of its home games and only a quarter of its away games in a three-year period. Further research by Schwartz and Barsky (1977), who looked at the outcomes of 1,880 major league baseball games, 182 professional football games, 542 professional hockey games and 1,485 college basketball games which took place in one year, discovered that there was a higher percentage of wins when the matches were played at home, for all types of sport. On average, of total wins, 59 per cent were played at home and 41 per cent were played away.

Figure 1.2 Supporting fans increase the players' motivation to win

'So what?', you may say. It's obvious that we are going to be more comfortable in our own familiar environments, but why?

This is where you need to assume that your reader knows nothing, and you must explain the findings to them in order to show that you have thought about and understood the meaning of such research. Environmentalists would say that the results may be caused by people feeling safer on their own territory. They are familiar with the surroundings and so they do not have to deal with finding their way around a new environment as well as having to prepare themselves for the match. This would mean that their level of arousal may well be lower than if they had to deal with both. You, of course, would realise that according to the Yerkes–Dodson Law (and the inverted-U hypothesis) arousal increases performance to a certain level, but over-arousal leads to a decrease in performance, which is why the people who were playing away lost more matches.

However, this isn't the only reason. At home matches, there are more team supporters and so the feelings of the crowd may well influence how well the team performs. After all, theories of audience effects suggest that if the audience is known to you, and is on your side, you will be less aroused than if you feel the audience is hostile or judgemental. To back up this idea, research by Cotterell *et al.* (1968) discovered that if an audience was blindfolded and couldn't see what the participants were doing, the audience effect disappeared. This indicates that we must be aware of how important the audience is to the performer, in terms of the audience's evaluation of his/her performance. In other words, the performer must be *aware* that the audience is evaluating his/her performance for the audience effect to occur. (We will assume at this point, that the performer won't consider the possibility of the audience having a 'reflex response' and cheering irrespective of their performance, but will simply see applause as support!)

In order to describe research effectively, ask yourself the questions shown in Figure 1.3.

HOW TO EVALUATE … ●●●●●●●●●●●●●●●●●●●●●●●●●●

The second requirement for most psychological examinations is to evaluate the work you have read – to consider both the strengths and weaknesses of the research. There are many different issues to consider when evaluating research, although it is not my intention to go into these in any detail at this point. That comes later in the book. However, at this point I want you to realise that evaluation is actually something that you are totally familiar with – it's just that you aren't always aware of what you are doing.

You probably remember how, when you were young and your parents told you something, you simply accepted that what they told you was true. As you got older you no doubt began to realise that your parents didn't always know everything and sometimes actually got it wrong. Similarly with teachers; when you were a child you

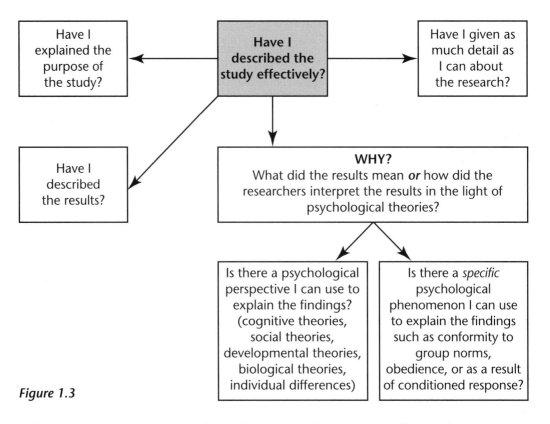

Figure 1.3

believed that they knew everything about everything. Did you find it disappointing that these adults, whom you initially believed to be infallible, were sometimes unable to answer a question, may have been somewhat opinionated, and on rare occasions were actually wrong?

Figure 1.4 *'Dad, that's not what you told me last week!'*

The first time it happened to me, I wasn't sure what to think. It involved not a teacher but my father. He was actually a very clever man and when I was a child I believed that he knew everything about everything. One day I came home from school and he asked me what I was studying at the time. In fact the subject I was studying was related to current news headlines and I was very interested in it. Consequently I had gone to the library to look up the topic (biology and cross-cultural differences). He started talking about the topic as if he were an authority on it, although what he was saying contradicted everything I had read. I then realised for the first time that information given by our elders isn't necessarily correct, and I felt quite disillusioned.

Another example of how we are fed misinformation comes from newspaper articles. I'm sure you have realised by now that many of the stories published are actually inaccurate to a lesser or larger extent, either intentionally or unintentionally. A story will present itself and the journalists may embellish it with one or two speculative details as if they were true. People then read the story, assume the speculations are true, and believe a story that bears little resemblance to what really happened. In fact in some cases, the misreporting is pure sensationalism in order to increase sales or provoke some kind of response. Similarly, the results of surveys can be suspect, for example the survey which claimed that one in five men are gay – which was conducted in Brighton! This can have two effects – either you start questioning *everything* or you carry on accepting all that you are told. However, if you do decide to question things, it's actually quite hard work because you have to think!

Psychology students are encouraged not to take information at face value, but to evaluate that information before deciding whether or not to accept it. The problem is, we don't always do this, especially when information we are told agrees with what we feel to be the case. But what if that information is startling or liable to change the way that society functions? Even with information that has this degree of importance, we do not always look at it objectively. Take, for example, genetic engineering and the potential to alleviate or eliminate many inherited diseases using gene therapy. Most people have an opinion on whether they think research in this area should go ahead or not. They are often influenced more by the opinions of family and friends, religious beliefs and so on, and seldom by factual evidence.

There are a large number of evaluative issues to be taken into consideration when looking at research done in the name of psychology. They are not simply the obvious ones such as the methodology or the ethics. What we must remember is that both individual pieces of research and psychological theories can have such an immense impact on people's lives that we need to feel confident that they are *effective* and *appropriate*. In fact most pieces of research are well planned and executed but some may be biased and others poorly designed and implemented. However, if you are aware of the weaknesses or biases in the findings, you can then make an informed choice as to whether you wish to accept or reject those findings. It may also inspire you to replicate or improve on them. As I said earlier, the other point to make is that when you evaluate something, you must look at both the positive and the negative points and be fair in your evaluation. Most research has good and bad points.

It is when we fail to look critically at research that we are in danger of making mistakes. This generally happens when we believe something to be true and either ignore evidence to the contrary, or misinterpret it. Let me give you an example. If you believe that television viewing influences how we behave, you will probably be very concerned about the amount of violent television that children have access to. You could support this idea by citing the fact that Bandura *et al.'s* (1961) demonstration that children learn aggressive behaviour by imitation, in this case by imitating the behaviour of an aggressive adult role model who is seen beating up a 'bobo' doll. However, recent evidence from Charlton (2000) has shown that the children on the South Atlantic island of St. Helena, who first received television in March 1995, have shown little change in their anti-social behaviour such as kicking, pushing and pinching. The only change that has been noticed is a small decrease in anti-social behaviour, even though they watch a slightly higher level of violence than we do in Britain.

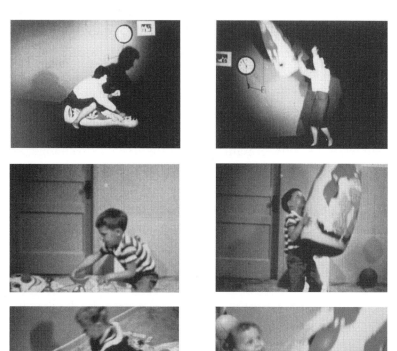

Figure 1.5 *Pictures from the Bandura* et al. *study. The top two photographs show an adult model and the other four show both a boy and a girl imitating what they have seen*

What should you do, in the face of evidence which seems to totally contradict what you believe? You could either change your opinion, or you could discredit the source of information by, for example, suggesting that the methodology used was flawed and biased. So where does this leave us? Well, it means that we must be prepared to look objectively (if that is possible) at all the information available to us, make our own decisions and be prepared to back up our conclusions with considered arguments and valid evidence and not simply state our feelings. We should not argue for argument's sake, and we must always be prepared to listen to new ideas that may contradict our original beliefs. If we do all this, then we are in a better position to judge psychological theories and evidence and apply them to everyday life.

As I said earlier, the evaluative issues mentioned below are covered in more detail in the following chapters, but Figure 1.6 gives you an idea of the kind of issues we will be considering.

Alternatively, if you are evaluating theories, you can use a similar technique including the questions shown in Figure 1.7.

COMPARING AND CONTRASTING ... • • • • • • • • • • • • •

When you evaluate psychological research, it helps if you can compare and contrast the research with other work that has been carried out by other psychologists – in fact in most branches of psychology you are expected to be able to do just that. By comparing one piece of research with another, you can look for similarities (comparisons) and differences (contrasts) between them and therefore draw a conclusion as to which, in your opinion, is most effective either in the methodology used, or as an explanation for a piece of behaviour.

Most students are perfectly capable of comparing and contrasting – in fact they do it on a regular basis although not always within psychology. I have given below a very simple example of how we compare and contrast features of our daily lives, as a way of 'demystifying' the terms.

Imagine you are going out to buy something to wear to a really special party. You are determined to get something that is suitable, fashionable, will look good on you and not be too expensive. The chances are you will have to go to a number of shops before you find something that meets all these criteria. You know what it's like – the really stunning clothes cost a fortune, the ones you quite like make you look gross, and the ones that feel comfortable look like tracksuits! You spend a lot of time wandering from shop to shop, trying on this and that, working out which outfit is the best one to buy. You are, in fact, comparing and contrasting the different outfits in a number of ways. Say you select three outfits and decide that they all make you look and feel good. You aren't too sure which one to go for so you look at the price tickets to see if that helps you make a decision. You find that two of them are extremely expensive. In fact, when you **compare** the prices, there is only a few pence difference between the expensive items – £105.95 and £105.99 – so their prices are very similar. However, in **contrast**, one is very reasonable – a price you can afford – so it is this difference in price which decides which outfit you are going to buy.

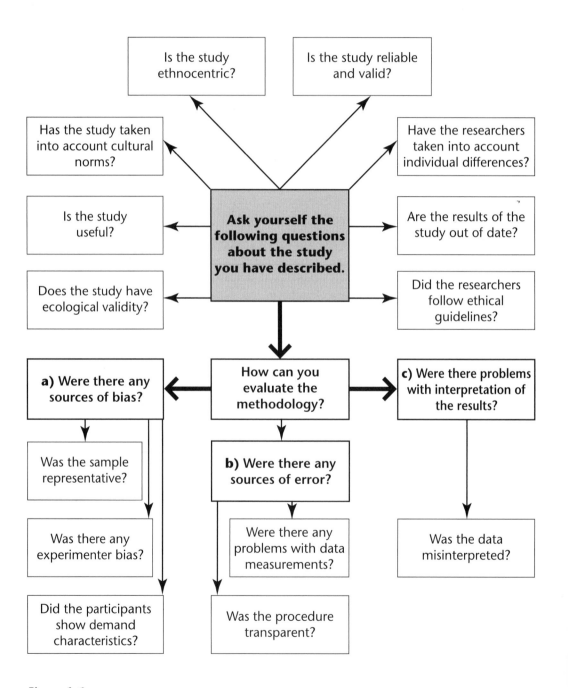

Figure 1.6

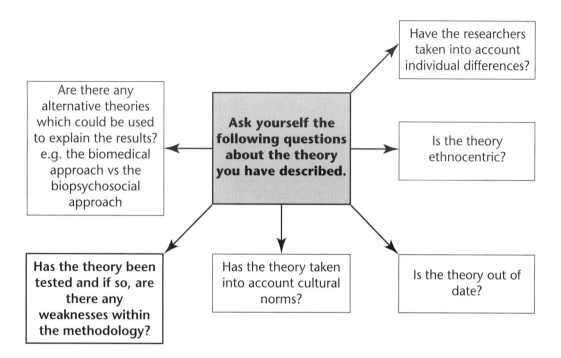

Figure 1.7

Now let's consider how this can be done using psychological examples and focusing on the nature of the sample used.

Below I have briefly described three pieces of research from the area of **health psychology**. (The first is also explored in another context in Chapter 5.)

John McKinlay (1975) investigated 'lower-class' women's understanding of 13 terms used in a maternity ward, such as 'breech', 'navel' and 'protein'. He found that on average only 39 per cent of patients understood the 13 words.

Bulpitt (1988, cited in Kaplan *et al.*, 1993) investigated the likelihood of compliance to health requests by investigating the use of treatments for hypertension in a group of men. He found that the medication prescribed to patients had improved the condition by reducing the symptoms of depression and headache, but it also had the side-effects of increased sexual problems, e.g. impotence and problems with ejaculation. The findings were that due to these side-effects, the patients were less likely to comply with medical advice.

Swigonski (1987) investigated the effects of social relationships on the likelihood of adherence to health requests. She studied a cross-section of kidney disease patients with varying numbers of social relationships and found that the more relationships these patients had, the more likely they were to fail to monitor their fluid intake, as advised by medical practitioners. She concluded that the more relationships the patients had, the more likely they were to take part in social gatherings where food and beverages would be present. The more opportunities that were offered to the kidney patients to take part in these gatherings, the harder they would find it to control the consumption of fluids.

If we consider the effects of the sample bias on the results of this research, we can compare and contrast the different samples in these pieces of research in order to understand the results. McKinlay's sample consists of 'lower-class' women only and **in comparison** Bulpitt's sample consists solely of men. These examples of gender bias should make you realise that the results are not generalisable to the population as a whole and that the results might have been very different if different genders had been used for each of the studies. It is possible to argue that if the second study had been conducted on women, they may have had far less of a problem with the sexual side-effects of the drug than the men. **In contrast**, Swigonski used a far more representative sample which had no gender bias and therefore the results are more likely to be generalisable to the population as a whole.

You should now have got the idea that comparing means that the issue is *true for two or more of the named studies* whilst contrasting means that the issue *applies to one study or theory but not the other.*

Now here is a much more complex example. See if you can identify the similarities in the first two pieces of research, and the difference in the last. These examples are taken from the area of **educational psychology**.

It has been argued that one of the factors that can influence the educational performance of children is their ability to use language.
Bernstein (1973) suggested that there are two forms of language, the restricted code and elaborated code. Bernstein claimed that some children are disadvantaged educationally because they experience a restricted vocabulary at home, consisting of brief phrases that are often context-dependent and more easily understood by those who share the social situation. The elaborated code, on the other hand, is more common to the middle classes, and is the code most frequently used in schools. Consequently, children who use the restricted code may find it hard to understand the instructions and explanations of the teachers and will therefore be seen as less able students.

In comparison, Tizard *et al.* (1983) compared the language used at home and school by two groups of girls aged between three and four. Half of the children were from 'uneducated' and half from 'educated' homes. The researchers found significant differences in the types of language used in the children's homes and noticed that the children from the working-class homes had to adjust their language style to suit that of the school whereas the middle-class children used the same style in both places. Tizard *et al.* argued that this would ultimately disadvantage the working-class children who would have to learn how to adapt.

In contrast, Hughes (1989) cited research that suggested teachers believed some children came from homes which failed to socialise them properly, especially in the use of language. The suggestion was that this failure in language use would leave them with a 'deficiency' and that this deficit would result in their being cognitively disadvantaged. This would manifest in a lack of socialisation and poor performance at school. However, the results of recording the same children at home contradicted these ideas. The children talked about a variety of topics with their parents, who corrected and guided them in their use of language (even though the grammatical corrections may not have been ideal). Therefore it appears that the situation had more impact on the children's linguistic skills than their class origin. When the same children were put in different contextual environments within the school setting, they demonstrated wide-ranging and diverse linguistic abilities. This indicated that perhaps class-based differences in language are not particularly important when it comes to educational achievement.

Here the work by Bernstein is being supported by that of Tizard *et al.*; therefore the findings of one piece of research can be **compared** to the findings of the next. They both support the idea that children from working-class homes would be disadvantaged when it came to understanding the language of the classroom, which tends to be more 'middle class' in nature. **In contrast**, the work by Hughes suggests that these language differences do not really exist, because when monitored at home, the children and their parents in the study demonstrated many different types of linguistic interactions which were far more sophisticated than the teachers expected. This would suggest that it is the nature of the child and the context of the situation that may result in differences in school performance rather than the type of language used within the home. Children who feel comfortable in certain settings may be more vocal, but the ones who are quiet or unwilling to voice their opinions may feel shy or lack confidence rather than being unable to understand others or express themselves effectively.

Hopefully these two examples give you an idea of what is meant by comparing and contrasting, as these are skills which will help you to gain good marks in any kind of psychology examination.

In order to compare and contrast research effectively, ask yourself the questions shown below.

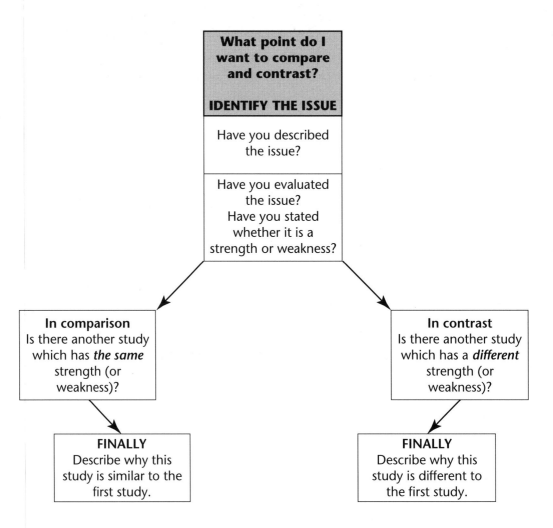

Figure 1.8

Explaining behaviours

2

> **How to answer the question 'Why?' when looking at the results of psychological research. Perspectives covered:**
>
> - **Cognitive**
> - **Developmental**
> - **Social**
> - **Biological**
> - **Individual differences (the idiographic approach)**

Most psychologists favour a certain type of explanation as to why behaviours occur; for example, some psychologists (of the developmental school) maintain that certain behaviours may be caused by the experiences we have while we grow up; others (biological psychologists) see them as a result of our physiology. Because they tend to focus on their own specific areas it doesn't mean that they discount *all* other explanations, they just tend to focus on their own. When you are learning about psychology, although you may have an area which you find most interesting, you generally look at *all* aspects of psychology. This means you are in a much better position to find the best explanation for a piece of behaviour rather than being biased in one direction or another.

Therefore if you are writing about a specific type of behaviour, you can try to explain it using perhaps one or two different perspectives. If you were evaluating what psychologists had found out about certain topic areas, you could also use a further alternative perspective to evaluate your original conclusion (and impress the examiner at the same time). Below is an overview of the different perspectives and at the end of these, I will give examples of how these can be used to explain behaviour and then how you can compare alternative explanations.

There are many books written specifically about all of these areas which explain the finer points in much more detail and far more effectively than I can. Of course, to understand them fully, you should try to take time to find out about different theorists and their work. However, I have tried to give a very brief, if somewhat superficial, overview of the different areas as we are more concerned here with using these perspectives to interpret the findings of applied psychology. Then at the end of the chapter, I have given a brief and simplistic example of how you can use these perspectives to explain a specific topic. I have taken the example of smoking, as this topic can be addressed by most of the theories.

THE COGNITIVE PERSPECTIVE ● ● ● ● ● ● ● ● ● ● ● ● ● ● ● ● ● ●

Cognitive psychologists focus on our mental processes or cognitions, trying to explain how they work and how they fit together and ultimately how they might direct our behaviour. The mental processes they focus on include memory, perception, attention, language, thought and the ability to problem solve. Cognitive psychologists rarely take into account other explanations of behaviour such as social psychological theories or biological explanations; instead they focus on the internal processes which involve performance at mental tasks. Therefore when interpreting research from a cognitive theoretical standpoint, you should consider the mental processing that was involved in the reasoning and decision-making of participants. This is not to be confused with the emotional feelings they have because, as we have said, cognitive psychology deals with seemingly rational thought rather than emotive behaviour.

Cognitive psychology 'took off' at the same time as the development of computers and the analogy between the brain and a computer allowed the first attempts to see mental processes as a kind of information-processing system which worked in a serial manner – with one thing happening after another, much the same way as computers process information. However, we are far more sophisticated than even the most advanced computer system and manage to process huge amounts of information at the same time – in parallel.

This limitation to the original analogy didn't actually deter cognitive psychology from developing because the desire to understand the internal mechanisms still remains. However, the way that the processing works is still frequently modelled on basic flow diagrams such as the multi-store model of memory originally proposed by Atkinson and Shiffrin in 1968, although nowadays they are somewhat more sophisticated.

Don't forget that when you look at information from a cognitive perspective you should consider the way that information is processed by the individual and the things that will affect the processing, such as past experiences and motivations.

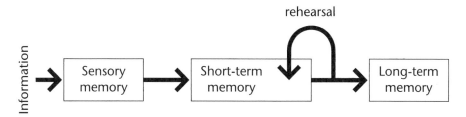

Figure 2.1 Atkinson and Shiffrin's multi-store model

Memory

The process which has the greatest bearing on the rest of our cognitive processes is our memory. We store previously learned information and we use that information to help us make decisions, to interpret, to understand and to identify what is going on. The problem is that memory is not like a tape recorder – it is a dynamic process that can be influenced by information received after an event. This was demonstrated by Loftus and Palmer (1974) when they used leading questions to show how it is possible to alter an original memory.

We generally remember things that are of personal relevance to us rather than every piece of information that is available and we use this information to make sense of new experiences. Schema theory provides a theoretical framework to explain how we organise this stored information into 'packages' which contain everything we know about certain topics. We then use these individual schema to help us make sense of a situation if parts of it are confusing or ambiguous. This helps to explain how two people can interpret the same situation differently because none of us, even identical twins, have identical schemata. Even though we may live very similar lives, they are never absolutely identical – we may have different friends, different teachers, different positions within our families. The structure and functioning of our memories may be similar but the content is often very diverse. These **individual differences** form the basis of the idiographic approach, covered later in this chapter.

Perception

Perception is the interpretation of the sensations we experience through all of our senses: taste, touch, smell, hearing and vision. Psychologists focus on visual perception more than any other area because eyes are responsible for taking in far more information than any of the other sense modalities in people with normal sight.

There are two different theories which relate to how we process visual information and it is probably worth mentioning them here. The first theoretical descriptions of how this processing occurs are the **bottom-up theories**, like those of Marr and

Gibson. They believe that there is enough information in the visual array alone to cause the stimulated cells at the back of the retina to produce sufficient neuronal firings to allow us to interpret what it is we have actually seen. However, if this was actually a good enough explanation of perception, this would mean that we would always see the same things as each other, and this is not the case. The Peter Paul Goblet, for example, can be seen as either a vase or two faces looking at each other. We are not sure what the object is and so we use stored information to help us interpret what we see. This is known as the **top-down theory** of perception, as suggested by Richard Gregory (1973) when he argued that we have to test hypotheses about what visual stimuli are, on the basis of our prior experiences and stored information.

This should make you realise that there is a strong link between perception and memory because how we interpret situations depends on our past experiences and these experiences are stored in our memories. An example of this is seeing a man wielding a machête coming into the room where we are sitting. We wouldn't try to find out if he was lost, we would immediately perceive him as a threat and would make a run for it because we know, from information stored in our memories, that machêtes and strange men tend to spell trouble!

Cognitive psychologists who are interested in perceptual abilities have focused on the differences in perception between groups of people, especially various cultural groups. Deregowski (1972), in his article on 'Pictorial perception and culture', drew together much of the information about the variations in perceptual abilities of different cultural groups and pointed out that these abilities related to past experiences. Evidence such as this indicates that we may well interpret events from different perspectives and these perspectives are called 'sets'. They have been illustrated by many researchers who have demonstrated that context will influence perception. Perhaps one of the most famous of these is the ambiguous number 13 that was demonstrated by Minturn and Bruner (1951). Here the expectation when you are reading the letters horizontally is that they are A B C. Whereas when you read them vertically, you would expect them to be 12, 13 and 14.

$$12$$
$$A \quad 13 \quad C$$
$$14$$

Figure 2.2

Remember that the way people see and interpret different things relates very much to their past experiences and this can help to explain their subsequent behaviour (top-down processing).

Attention

Interpretation implies that we have actually paid enough attention to the information in the first place to begin to process it in any way. Cognitive psychologists have investigated the area of attention, trying to find out what catches our attention and how much information we can attend to at any one time. Theories have looked at the nature of the stimulus with research by Broadbent (1958) suggesting that we attend to information purely on the basis of its physical characteristics. By this he meant that if a noise is very loud, we will pay attention to it even though it may not be of interest to us. However, later research suggested that this wasn't the case. After all, have you ever been in a situation where there is a continuous loud noise, but after a while you cease to hear it – you *habituate* to it (that is, you get so used to it that you end up being able to ignore it).

Other studies of attention have focused on the difference between **selective** attention and **divided** attention (Allport *et al.*, 1972; Shaffer, 1975; Shiffrin and Schneider, 1977). We are quite able to divide our attention between a number of different stimuli if we are familiar with them, but what happens when they are unfamiliar? When we start to learn to drive, for instance, it takes all of our attention just to cope with all the things we have to do (selective attention). Later, when driving is a well-practised skill, we can do all manner of things at the same time (divided attention). So the strangeness or familiarity of a task can influence our performance of it.

Theory of mind

Most people understand that other people have thoughts and beliefs that are different from their own; that is, they have a 'theory of mind'. Baron Cohen, Leslie and Frith (1985) demonstrated that not everyone has a theory of mind; in fact, it is one of the more common deficits in autism whereby autistic people are unable to 'mind read', to sense what another is thinking or feeling. This ability to understand that someone else has a different mind to our own is a developmental achievement and is generally shown by the time children reach five years of age. However, some people never seem to achieve the ability to understand the mind of another person, or perhaps just choose not to. To understand the motives for behaviour, it is necessary to consider that most of us find it difficult to ignore what we believe someone else is feeling, and this may well dictate how we behave towards them. Perhaps an exception to this rule are psychopaths who seem to lack emotions. We might argue that their lack of attention to the feelings of others shows that they, too, lack a theory of mind. However, it is more likely that they probably *do* understand how other people feel, but simply don't care.

Language

Every child brought up in an interactive environment learns language and is usually extremely fluent and competent by the age of five. However, according to the sociologist Basil Bernstein (1961), language is a social rather than individual phenomenon. By this he meant that the language we learn reflects the social group in which we grow up. If we accept the argument proposed by Edward Sapir and Benjamin Lee Whorf (1941) that language actually dictates how we think, we need to be aware that without the relevant language, we cannot actually perceive or think about something. As we saw in Chapter 1, Bernstein suggested that children from working-class backgrounds learned what he described as the restricted code of language. This is language which, according to Gross is:

> 'grammatically crude, repetitive, rigid, limited in its use of adjectives and adverbs, uses more pronouns than nouns, and involves short, grammatically simple and incomplete sentences. It is context-bound; that is, the meaning is not made explicit but assumes the listener is familiar with the situation being described. For example, a conversation might start with the words 'He gave me it', when the listener cannot be expected to know who 'he' or what 'it' is. 'I' is rarely used and much of the meaning is conveyed non-verbally.
>
> By contrast, the elaborated code is grammatically more complex and flexible, sentences are longer and more complex. It makes use of a range of subordinate clauses, as well as conjunctions, prepositions, adjectives and adverbs, and allows the expression of abstract thoughts. 'I' is often used, more nouns than pronouns are used and it is context-independent so that it does not assume the listener is familiar with the situation being described but makes the meaning explicit (for example, 'John gave me this book')'.

Gross (1992), p368

Obviously this will have consequences for children in terms of disadvantaging them both socially and, more relevantly, educationally. It may also determine the nature of their interactions and understanding within the adult world, and influence the way they deal with problems and tasks they are set. After all, if you don't actually understand what is expected of you, how can you do your best?

Some key concepts of cognitive psychology
- Memory is not like a tape recorder.
- Memory can be influenced by the nature of a question or by past experiences or knowledge (schemas).
- We don't all see the same thing in the same way.

- Expectation or past experience will influence what we actually perceive.
- We can't always pay attention to everything in our environment so we attend to the things that are more unfamiliar or of interest to us.
- Most people understand that other people have thoughts and beliefs that are different to our own (a theory of mind).
- The nature of the language we use may well be influenced by our background and past experiences (as well as our stage of development).

Therefore in order to explain behaviour in terms of cognitive theories, apply the following questions to the study:

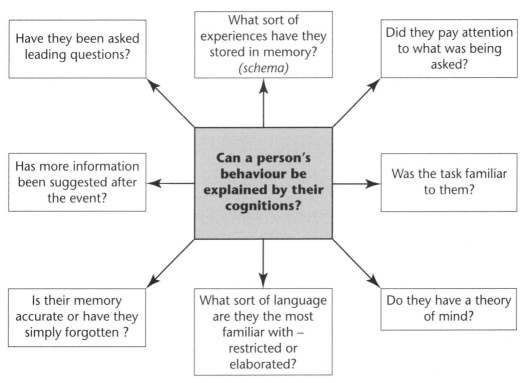

Figure 2.3

THE DEVELOPMENTAL PERSPECTIVE ● ● ● ● ● ● ● ● ● ● ● ●

There are a number of different developmental theories which seek to explain different aspects of the process of child development. Some of the theories are cognitive in nature and focus on **cultural universals**, those developmental milestones, achieved by all children, from all cultures, indicating that some aspects of development are innate. Some are psychodynamic (relate to Freud) and others are social theories which suggest that the early social experiences we have will influence our later pattern of behaviours and relationships. Each theory not only helps to explain the milestones children pass through but can also help to give us an insight into adult behaviour. It is not my place here to go into all the theories of child development or the research on which they are based. I have simply focused on the ones which may be most useful in terms of explaining later behaviour, and also the ones which are most familiar to students of psychology.

Cognitive developmental theory

This theory suggests that when we are very young, we are not capable of the same ability to think, reason and problem-solve as adults. We have to go through a process of cognitive development in order to achieve the abilities of an adult. Piaget is the most well-known cognitive developmentalist and he believed that there are a set number of stages, which are cumulative and age-related, and that all children go through them in the same order: therefore they are *innate*. He also believed that children are active problem-solvers, so that if placed in the right environment, with interesting educational toys and ways of investigating the properties of the environment, they will almost teach themselves. The way that children take in the information relating to the world around them is by assimilating and accommodating the information into their schemas, and it is these which dictate their manipulation of mental processing at a later age.

There are of course other theories, notably that of Vygotsky who did not completely agree with Piagetian reasoning. Vygotsky (1896–1934) lived in Russia but his work was not readily available in translation outside the Soviet Union until the 1960s. He claimed that we need to direct children and facilitate their learning in a more interactionist way than that suggested by Piaget, and that without this direction, children's cognitive development would be far less impressive.

Although these, and other cognitive developmental theories are not always in total agreement, all would suggest that if a child were raised in a situation where they had little or no stimulation from others, no verbal interaction, few toys and little means of finding out about the properties of the world, its cognitive development would be very slow. The child would then be disadvantaged when it came to abstract thinking and reasoning and therefore be less able to work out the long-term consequences of their actions.

Learning theories

As children we are all subjected to different environments and different experiences and we learn from each of these many different patterns of behaviour. We learn things such as our respective gender roles, how to behave in a given situation, how to interact with others, how to look, how to demonstrate our skills and so on. It is partly because we all have different experiences as we grow up that we are all unique – even children from the same family will turn out differently because of the social experiences they have, their positions in the family as oldest or youngest children and so on.

There are two main learning theories, conditioning and social learning theory.

Conditioning has two forms, **classical** and **operant**. Classical conditioning (Pavlov, 1927) involves producing a reflex response to a new stimulus such as occurs in developing a phobia or irrational fear. These forms of learning tend to be spontaneous and therefore unconscious. Operant conditioning (Skinner, 1938), on the other hand, is where we learn to do something in response to something else because we know that we will be rewarded (reinforced), either by others (extrinsically) or by self-congratulation (intrinsically). Operant techniques of learning are with us throughout our lives; we work hard at school to get gold stars or merit points, we study for our A Levels because passing them will mean we get to university. We learn how to be productive in our jobs in order to get well paid, and so on.

It is worth noting that we can also learn undesirable behaviours if they are reinforced. If a child is ignored by its parent and the only way it can get attention is by being a real pain in the neck, it may become naughty and destructive in order to be noticed. What will make that behaviour worse is if the parent then buys it sweets to shut it up; it will have learned an inappropriate behaviour because it was rewarded (reinforced) by sweets.

Social learning theory is an approach which was suggested by Albert Bandura and Robert Walters. They believe that we learn by the observation of role models and then imitate what we have seen, especially if the role model is seen to get some kind of reinforcement for their behaviour. As a result of the research undertaken by Bandura, Ross and Ross (1961) the conclusion was made that we are more likely to imitate a same sex role model who is seen as more powerful than we are.

Psychodynamic theory

Theories of child development are incomplete without referring to Freud's psychodynamic theory. Although Freud ultimately came to believe that we are biologically driven by life and death instincts (Eros and Thanatos), it is our early experiences up to the age of five years that will shape our personality for the rest of our lives. Freud believed that we pass through a number of different stages as we develop, notably the oral, anal and phallic stages, the latter of which ends at about the age of five. According to Freud, if we have any problems as we pass through a stage, we may well become stuck (or fixated) there and this will result in maladaptive behaviours as an adult.

Freud also suggests that there are a number of other features which may influence our behaviour in later life and can therefore be used to explain adult behaviours. These may concern memories that have been repressed into the unconscious or an imbalance in the three elements of our psyche. Below I have given a brief explanation of how this may happen.

The unconscious

Sometimes the way we behave is quite irrational, and makes people question why we have produced such bizarre or uncharacteristic behaviours. Freud suggested that the reason for this is because a huge amount of our past experiences are buried in our unconscious and can still influence our decisions and the way we behave. In fact, Freud (1901) claimed that about four-fifths of the mind are inaccessible to conscious awareness. One way of describing this model of the mind is to imagine an iceberg whereby four-fifths are under water level and only a fifth above. The fifth above water is the part of the mind of which we are aware, which suggests we don't really know ourselves. Freud suggested that there is a layer (just below water level) to which we have access when required and he called this the preconscious mind, but he maintained that the largest part was the unconscious mind which contains disturbing or emotionally painful memories.

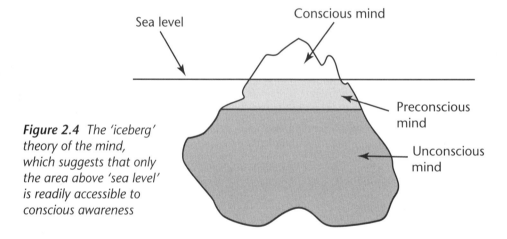

Figure 2.4 The 'iceberg' theory of the mind, which suggests that only the area above 'sea level' is readily accessible to conscious awareness

The structure of the psyche

Freud claims that the psyche is composed of three parts, the **id**, the **ego** and the **superego**. The id operates on the pleasure principle, and is present when we are born. It consists of primitive desires and primaeval urges to satisfy this need for pleasure, and these desires and urges are often reflexes, so contain no logical or rational thought. The id is the part of our personality which demands gratification and its desires are difficult to ignore.

The ego is the next part of the personality to develop and operates according to what is known as the reality principle. As we start to operate in the real world, we begin to realise that we can't always have what we want when we want it. We therefore work out ways of getting what we want. Perhaps we will have to wait, to 'defer gratification', for example. We learn from our experiences and our interactions with others. The ego has no moral component – it doesn't consider the moral rights and wrongs of behaving in certain ways, although, because of the dictates of the reality principle, it does take into account what is and isn't acceptable to other people.

The last part of the personality to develop is the superego which is in effect our moral principles. It develops as we start to internalise the rules and regulations of our parents and the society in which we live, so it becomes a kind of 'internal parent'. This superego comes from our progression through the Oedipus or Electra complexes and is, according to Freud, taken from our same-sex parent.

Freud says the ego's job is to maintain a state of dynamic equilibrium between these three parts. It has the position of trying to balance them out and to satisfy the demands of both the id and the superego in a realistic way.

It is easy to see how inequalities between the components of the psyche can lead to neurosis or personality disorders. Some people are dominated by either their id, becoming entirely selfish in their demands, or by their superego, being so moralistic that they cease to have any fun. According to Freud, if we can identify someone who has a weak ego, or an over-strict superego, we are on the way to helping them restore the balance which will make them function effectively.

Defence mechanisms

Freud believed that the unconscious parts of the mind are always trying to break through into conscious awareness but are kept in place by the ego (which explains why, if you have a weak ego, you are more likely to suffer with emotional problems). Freud suggested that the ego uses a number of defence mechanisms in order to assist it, although we are unaware of the process, three of which are listed below.

- We may use the mechanism of **repression**, which is where the conscious mind expels things which are too painful to remember, and keeps them buried in the unconscious where they remain, undetected, thus reducing our anxiety levels. However, these memories may continue to influence our behaviour in ways which may not seem connected, perhaps causing mental or psychosomatic symptoms, or resurfacing in dreams.
- If we are aware of a danger but find it too painful to acknowledge that awareness or decide that the way of dealing with it is too difficult, we may use **denial** as a defence mechanism.
- We may project our innermost weaknesses or unconscious wishes onto another person and blame them for what we are guilty of ourselves. **Projection** is the externalisation of our feelings onto another person (such as accusing someone of lying if we frequently lie ourselves).

Principles of therapy

Sometimes people become fixated in some stage of their childhood development and fail to reach the stage of dynamic equilibrium. This condition may result in a neurosis, which is an anxious mental state, and this can manifest as an anxiety disorder such as agoraphobia (a fear of open spaces), or depression. In order to overcome these problems patients may undergo psychoanalytic therapy, the aim of which is to help them gain access to the unconscious, deal with the issues and finally return to a state of dynamic equilibrium. Freud believed that repression was central to the development of a neurosis and that if we could gain access to repressed memories in a safe and non-threatening situation (in the psychoanalytic setting), this would allow us to face up to that memory and deal with it in a new and non-threatening way. Because the repressed memories may concern some part of our childhood, the patient is assisted to gain insight into the conflicts that may have occurred during development, and to therefore resolve these conflicts.

Attachment theory

The idea of attachment theory originated with John Bowlby, a psychotherapist who believed in the ideas of Freud. Bowlby maintained that 'mother love in infancy and childhood is as important for mental health as are vitamins and proteins for physical health' (Bowlby, 1953). He also claimed that the baby has to form an attachment to its mother during the first two years of life and that this was the critical period. If this bond were not developed during this time, there could be dire consequences for the social, emotional and intellectual development of the child, to the extent that they may well become an 'affectionless psychopath'.

Although many of Bowlby's ideas about how our early experiences with relationships are likely to influence the pattern of later relationships are accurate, he was a little extreme. Mother is not the crucial person – research has shown that a permanent and responsive caretaker of either sex is just as good. However, it makes sense to think that if we do learn from our early experiences, and if one of the first things we learn is that there is no one around to care for us or give us unconditional love, we will have no 'prototype' for relationships in later life. We may also end up believing that we are relatively worthless (because there is no one there for us), and we may have learned that we are helpless (because no matter what we do, everyone ignores our cries). These are good predictors of pathological adult behaviour such as depression and dysfunctional relationships. Hodges and Tizard (1989) demonstrated the effects of early experiences on later relationships in the last part of their longitudinal study and illustrated that the children who had disrupted early relationships had more problems at school when it came to relationships with peers and adults.

Some key concepts of developmental psychology:

- Children are not born with the same abilities as an adult, therefore they must be partly due to maturation and partly due to learning.
- Children learn certain behaviours – there are two theories of learning (conditioning and social learning theory).
- Children will continue to do things if their behaviour is reinforced.
- Children's role models have a large impact on their behaviour.
- Maternal deprivation may have an influence on the quality of relationships later in life.
- Extremely painful childhood experiences may be repressed into the unconscious but affect later thoughts or behaviour.
- According to Freud, progression through the Oedipus/Electra conflict may be necessary to form a strong moral conscience in the form of a 'superego'.

Therefore in order to explain behaviour in terms of developmental theories, apply the following questions to the study:

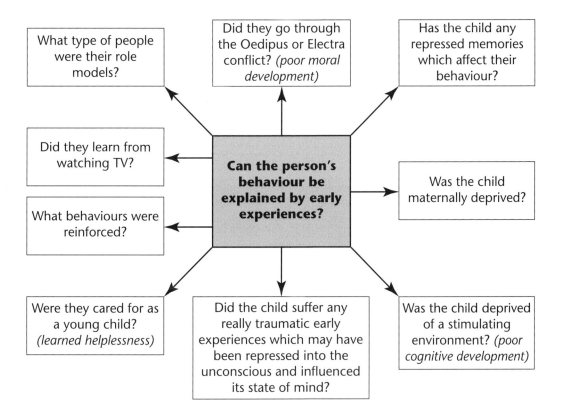

Figure 2.5

THE SOCIAL PERSPECTIVE ● ● ● ● ● ● ● ● ● ● ● ● ● ● ● ● ● ● ●

Social psychologists take the view that humans are naturally social creatures who have a biological need to interact with others. Therefore it would make sense to explain certain behaviours on the basis of our need for satisfactory social interactions rather than looking at individuals as isolated units. However, in order to interact successfully, we need to think about those interactions, and try to make sense of them. To do this we use stored information from past experiences to help us predict the outcome. Often behaviour may seem irrational or irresponsible, but if we take a broad overview of the behaviour in a social context, it sometimes becomes much more clear why a person has behaved in the way they have.

In-group/out-group behaviour

First of all – think of the way that we like to be part of a group and how we want to believe that our group is the best one around in order to make ourselves feel good. Tajfel (1970) demonstrated how strong this desire to discriminate against another group in favour of our own can be. He randomly grouped young boys without telling them who shared their group and found that they still showed in-group preferences when asked to allocate rewards.

Conforming

Next add the idea of conforming to group norms – if we want to belong to a group, we will usually conform to its norms in order to be accepted. This need for conformity is so great that it can be used to explain some unexpected results of research. Sometimes people do things we would not expect them to do, in order to conform to the norms of the experimental group they have been put in.

Roles

This conforming to group norms may involve taking on some kind of role. If we dress someone up in a uniform, they may behave in an uncharacteristic way just to fit in with the group. Zimbardo (1973) showed this when the participants in his prison simulation study became extremely nasty and authoritarian. Roles are very useful to indicate to us how to behave and to help us predict behaviours. On the other hand, role playing can also have quite negative consequences, especially if the perception of the role is incorrect. For example, when taking part in psychological research, people sometimes behave in the way they *believe* they are supposed to behave as a research participant. They are therefore responding to **demand characteristics**.

Obedience

Milgram (1963) showed how the majority of people are extremely obedient to authority figures, even going against their own conscience, if they perceive that authority to be legitimate. This level of obedience can sometimes explain strange or unexpected behaviours in research because people do not like to feel uncomfortable or anxious and so being obedient is often a way to reduce the level of anxiety.

Why people choose to act or not to act

Attributions

There are a number of theories seeking to explain why people choose to get involved in 'helping' situations. It seems to be the case that we are generally willing to help another person if we believe that the reason they need help is not through their own fault. Nisbett, Caputo, Legant and Marecek (1973) looked at how we explain our own behaviour and the behaviour of others. We tend to make what are known as 'dispositional attributions' to others, believing that their behaviour is due to some enduring personal characteristic they possess such as being a drunkard or a lazy good-for-nothing with no will power! However, we tend to make 'situational attributions' to ourselves – that is explaining or justifying our behaviour purely as a result of the situation we find ourselves in, such as:

> 'It wasn't my fault that I was done for drink driving. I was pressurised into having one at the firm's Christmas party and then got stopped by the police on the way home. I wouldn't drink under normal circumstances'.

Cost–benefit analysis

Another reason why people may decide to become involved in a situation is as a result of their weighing up the costs and benefits of participation. This cost–benefit analysis is known as social exchange theory and was proposed by Thibaut and Kelley in 1959. What happens is that we decide if we are going to get something out of our action (reward) and how much that action may cost or inconvenience us (cost). If we take one from the other and are still left with a positive value or profit, we are likely to become involved.

Diffusion of responsibility

It is very easy to share the responsibility for an event or action between the people who are present at the time. This phenomenon, known as diffusion of responsibility, can often explain why people choose not to take action if they are in a group but would do so if they were alone, even though they are well aware of what is going on. This is not the same as **dissolution of responsibility**, which is a better description of what happens when there are other witnesses, but their behaviour cannot be observed. We can therefore rationalise that someone else will probably have done something to help and so we do not need to get involved.

Pluralistic ignorance is often mistaken for dissolution of responsibility. Pluralistic ignorance occurs when people are unaware of the exact nature of the situation and so take their cues from the behaviour of others. They then redefine the situation in order to make sense of the information they have, even if their conclusion is actually incorrect.

Cognitive dissonance

When we hold two opinions or attitudes which are in conflict with each other, it can make us feel uncomfortable. This discomfort is known as cognitive dissonance. We don't like being in a state of cognitive dissonance; we would prefer cognitive consonance (or balance). Therefore we can either remove the attitude we feel less strongly about, or introduce a third belief to try and justify holding the other two. Festinger and Carlsmith (1959) demonstrated this when they asked students to tell someone that a task they had just completed was really interesting, when in fact it was absolutely mind-blowingly boring. The only way they seemed to be able to deal with having to lie was to convince themselves that it wasn't really that boring after all. This kind of justification is present in all our lives – we justify why we do things, even if the justification isn't the real reason, in order to not feel anxiety.

Smoking is probably the best example here:

I smoke *(first belief)*

I know that there is evidence which proves that smoking is bad for my health *(second belief)*

I therefore either stop smoking *(which is removing one of the attitudes or beliefs)*

or

discredit the evidence *(introduce a third belief)*

or

justify my smoking by saying I smoke only socially/low-tar cigarettes *(introduce an alternative third belief)*.

Using the ideas of cognitive dissonance, we can sometimes explain why people often behave in a way that seems to contradict what we know to be their opinions. It also helps us to understand why they may change their attitudes.

Some key concepts of social psychology:

- People like to be part of a group and see that group as better than other groups.
- People conform to group norms.
- People have a good understanding of role-related behaviour.
- People are often very obedient.
- People attribute situational reasons for behaviour to themselves but dispositional reasons to others.
- People weigh up the costs and benefits of their behaviour before they decide to get involved.
- People tend to share responsibility for a situation with others (diffuse responsibility).
- If someone is not sure what is going on, they will look to others to help them define the situation as an emergency or not (pluralistic ignorance).
- If someone holds two conflicting beliefs, they will either get rid of the weaker belief or introduce a third to make it possible to hold the other two (justify their reasons) and reduce cognitive dissonance.

Therefore in order to explain behaviour in terms of social psychological theories, apply the questions shown in Figure 2.6 to the study.

THE BIOLOGICAL PERSPECTIVE ● ● ● ● ● ● ● ● ● ● ● ● ● ● ●

Biopsychology focuses on the relationship between our anatomy (the structure of our bodies), our physiology (the way we work) and our behaviour. It seeks to explain behaviour in terms of the biological functioning of the body or biochemical changes in the brain. In fact most biopsychologists focus specifically on the brain and the nervous system although the glands and hormones also have some influence on our emotions. Biopsychology is really the other side of the nature–nurture debate – it looks at how important our physiology is to the way that we act in society rather than considering the experiences we have as forces shaping our behaviour.

Although it is often tempting to try to use the purely psychological to explain human behaviour, we are still biological 'specimens'. Therefore we must not ignore our biological components because they do have an influence on the way that we choose to act. Structural damage or abnormality, for example, can influence certain behaviours but there are also more subtle factors that affect the way that we behave, often without our conscious awareness.

The nervous system

The nervous system consists of two parts, the central nervous system (CNS), composed of the brain and spinal cord, and the peripheral nervous system (PNS) which

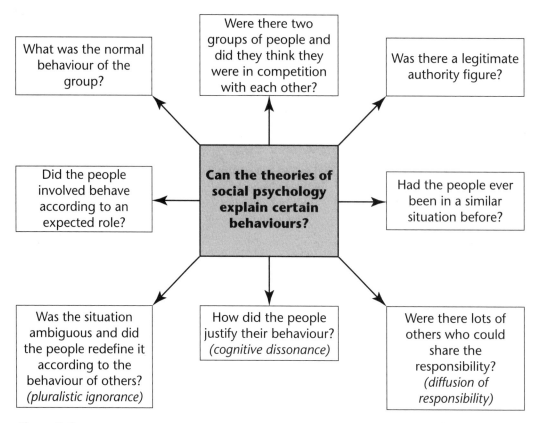

Figure 2.6

consists of a network of neurones located around the whole of the body. The CNS is the control centre for all the activities of the body, where information received is processed and there is coordination of actions and reactions both conscious and unconscious. The PNS is responsible for carrying information from the external world to the CNS and from the CNS back to the different parts of the body.

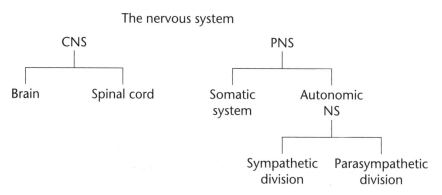

Figure 2.7 *The nervous system*

The PNS is subdivided into the somatic nervous system, which produces conscious responses, and the autonomic nervous system (ANS), which is the automatic self-regulating part which controls our rate of respiration and heart rate. The ANS is further subdivided into the sympathetic division, which is responsible for the fight or flight mechanism that speeds up bodily systems and prepares us for activity (so it has an excitatory function), and the parasympathetic division which is responsible for slowing the body down again and allowing bodily functions to return to their original state (so it is inhibitory).

The brain (structures and chemistry)

Structures

The brain consists of millions and millions of neurones which form a complex network in which different areas are responsible for different things. It is divided into two contralateral hemispheres, the left hemisphere controlling most of the right-hand side of the body, and the right hemisphere controlling the left-hand side.

Each hemisphere has the equivalent of three layers, the hindbrain, the midbrain and the forebrain (which contains the cerebral cortex), all of which sit on the brainstem (or reptilian brain) which controls our most basic functions such as respiration. As we evolved, we developed more and more neural layers and so the greater the intelligence, the larger and more layered the brain. The outer layer, or cerebral cortex, is the one which is of most interest to us as it is the one which is responsible for higher-order functioning such as complex thought processes, memories and the ability to plan and solve problems. Consequently, damage to or malfunction of the structures of our brain impairs our ability to think and rationalise in the normal way, which in turn may affect our behaviour.

Chemistry

Neurones, the cells of the nervous system, communicate by means of neurotransmitters. These are chemical messengers that change the polarity of the neurone's surface, making it more susceptible to carrying impulses generated within the nervous system. In simpler terms, they are the substances which allow the electrical impulses to travel from one neurone to the next. Different neurotransmitters are found in different parts of the nervous system, and the level of neurotransmitter will influence the behaviour of the person. To explain this in a little more detail – we have a 'normal' level of neurotransmitter, which makes us work with optimum efficiency. However, on occasion there may be a disturbance within the body due to illness, malfunction or drug-taking, which influences the level of neurotransmitter available, either increasing or decreasing it. This in turn either speeds up or slows down the speed of message transmission, making the person either overactive or depressed, or alternatively it may inhibit their cognitive functioning. The results of neurotransmitter disturbances can be seen in the following examples:

- Dopamine excess is related to schizophrenia whereby thoughts become excessive in number resulting in disorganised thinking.
- Serotonin decrease occurs with lack of daylight and this can cause depressed mood in some people susceptible to seasonal affective disorder (SAD).
- Acetylcholine is found in many synapses in the brain and spinal cord, especially in an area of the brain called the hippocampus which is involved in the formation of new memories. Cells producing acetylcholine degenerate in people suffering from Alzheimer's disease, and the consequent decrease in the production of acetylcholine results in loss of memory and cognitive functioning.
- LSD (which mimics serotonin thus increasing 'serotonin' levels) gives people a totally unreal perception of what is going on. Some people have, in the belief that they could fly, thrown themselves off buildings and fallen to their death.

Bearing in mind that there are over forty different types of neurotransmitters found in different areas of the body, these examples show that changes in the environment, activities, experience and health may all influence the way a person functions.

Arousal and stress

The body requires a constant internal environment in order for optimal functioning. As stated earlier, the homeostatic mechanisms responsible for maintaining this equilibrium are controlled by the autonomic nervous system. If we are unable to return to a balanced state, either due to the continued presence of the stimulus, or because of some malfunction of the autonomic nervous system, we will initially suffer from some kind of decrement (decline) in performance. Let me give you an example. If you are really worried or anxious about an examination, you know that you will not manage to perform as well as you would if you were sitting at home, in the safety of your own bedroom, feeling quite calm. The anxiety seems to affect the way that we think – thoughts become muddled, things get forgotten, and the more anxious you get, the worse the situation becomes. I remember being so worried about one of my final exams in psychology, that I sat for three-quarters of an hour writing nothing because I couldn't get my thoughts straight.

The idea that arousal affects behaviour was first suggested by Yerkes and Dodson in 1908. They were investigating the effect of giving rats electric shocks to their feet (thus making them anxious) on their ability to carry out discrimination tasks. The results of these and other studies resulted in the Yerkes–Dodson Law, which states that there is a relationship between the level of arousal and the level of performance, whereby it seems that we need some arousal to make us perform to our optimum, but when we get too aroused, performance declines. This has been illustrated by what is known as the inverted U-shaped curve.

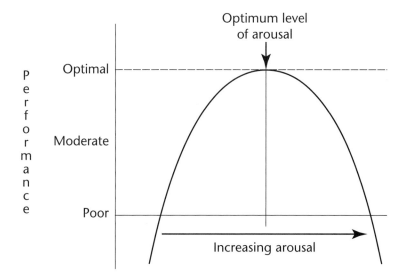

Figure 2.8 *The inverted U-shaped curve of the Yerkes–Dodson law*

Here you can see that with increased arousal, performance first of all improves but ultimately begins to decline, with performance tailing off the higher the arousal.

Yerkes and Dodson proposed that the level of arousal and its influence on maximum performance will depend on how good we are at the task. If it was a task that we found easy or one that we were confident with, then it would take more to get us 'over-aroused' than if the task were unfamiliar and we were nervous anyway.

The long-term effects of over-arousal on our behaviour are also significant. If we have remained over-aroused for a long period of time and are unable to return to a state of equilibrium due to the nature of the stressor, the inevitable result will be the gradual breakdown of the body's state of health. This continued state of over-arousal or prolonged anxiety will eventually lead to stress-related illness and can ultimately result in death.

Perhaps you are now beginning to realise that it is essential for us to consider every theoretical perspective in order to help us to understand the complexity of human behaviour. The influences our physiology has on our behaviour extend beyond the actual structural influences. I remember, when I was younger, finding my parents very irritating and I always vowed I would never be like them. The trouble is, I often hear myself saying what they said to me, which could possibly be put down to mimicry or simply learned patterns of behaviour. The worst part is that I sometimes look in the mirror and see certain mannerisms or expressions which are so much like those of my parents. I also have handwriting very similar to my mother's and seem to enjoy the same kinds of things she enjoys. Bearing in mind I left home when I was 17, and haven't seen huge amounts of her over the years as we live so far away from each other, I can't believe it is all learned – how frightening! I also see my daughters reproducing family mannerisms. My eldest daughter is the image of her natural father in terms of sense of humour and facial expressions and yet she grew up with a stepfather.

Therefore we must also consider any potentially inherited factors. After all, we are a product of our genes, and although the environment can have a strong influence in terms of learned patterns of behaviour, our personality and intelligence, for example, may well have a genetic component. In fact, there is great interest in biological theories of behaviour at present, with the advent of the Human Genome Project. The next chapter deals specifically with the topic of behavioural genetics as this is one area where much research is focused at the present time. Again, it is only a very brief overview of an extremely complex topic, but it should help us to move us on from the original nature–nurture dichotomy to a slightly more sophisticated level of understanding of how biological factors influence our behaviour. In the meantime we will consider the more familiar areas of biopsychology in order to help explain behaviour.

Reductionism

You must also be aware that biological theories are also linked to the philosophical perspective of **reductionism** – this means reducing explanations to the most basic level. For instance, a reductionist view of the purpose of relationships is that we need to send our genes forth into the next generation. This ignores other reasons like the fact that the person is actually really nice/good fun/attractive/likes us and so on. An advantage of reductionist views is that if we reduce explanations to the most fundamental level possible, we are less likely to overlay those explanations with more subjective and possibly inaccurate theories. The problem with the reductionist viewpoint is that it sometimes oversimplifies behaviour and actually distracts us from understanding the overall functioning of the human animal. An example of this is that the way an individual neurone may function when observed in isolation is not necessarily indicative of how it functions in the body, in conjunction with many other excitatory or inhibitory neurones. Now apply this to people – how an individual functions alone is very different from how people function in groups (think of the studies of conformity and group behaviour).

Species-specific behaviour

There is considerable evidence that all our behaviour is simply a result of our biological make-up. This has been demonstrated with animal research, principally because it is impossible to research human beings in the same way. An example of how behaviour has a biological basis is shown by behaviour which is species-specific. Mating behaviours are classic examples of species-specific behaviour. Prairie chickens, native to the upper Midwest area of the USA, conduct an elaborate mating ritual, described by Joseph McInerney (1999) as 'a sort of line dance for birds, with spread wings and synchronised group movements'. Tinbergen (1952) carefully investigated the three-spined stickleback that makes its 'nest' in river beds. However, there is a black stickleback that has twelve spines that makes its nest in the weeds growing in ponds and rivers and it has a totally different pattern of mating behaviour. In fact it seems that some behaviours are so characteristic of particular species that biologists use them to help differentiate between closely related species.

Figure 2.9 Three-spined stickleback

My border collie displays a good example of species-specific behaviour. She goes into 'rounding up' mode whenever she sees anything that looks like it could be herded – horses, chickens, even small children. Retrievers, springer spaniels and Labradors make idea gun-dogs as they retrieve prey.

In humans, it seems that some behaviours run in families. For example, there is evidence that some mental illnesses are inherited and these mental illnesses result in certain types of behaviour. In fact geneticists have managed to create or extinguish certain types of behaviours in mice. They have inserted extra genes or disabled others and this has lead to cases such as the wiping out of the nurturing behaviours of mice, to producing a mouse strain called a 'twirler' that continuously goes round in a circle.

Figure 2.10 *The Twirler produces bizarre, uncharacteristic behaviour due to gene manipulation*

Brain damage

Evidence has also shown that people's behaviour can change dramatically in response to some kind of damage to their physiological workings. Phineas Gage was a prime example of a man who had been an amiable and well-mannered person prior to sustaining brain damage. Once he had sustained such immense damage to his frontal cortex, he became rude and obnoxious and his behaviour lacked the normal social restraints. Sperry (1968) demonstrated in his study of people who had 'split-brains' that under certain circumstances, they were unable to respond to visual stimuli in the same way as 'normals'. Differences in glucose metabolism was found in the brains of defendants who had pleaded not guilty to murder on the grounds of insanity, compared with the control group (Raine *et al.*, 1997) and this may have been part of the reason why their behaviour was so extreme.

Drugs and emotions

Schachter and Singer (1962) demonstrated that the chemicals in drugs can affect the way that people feel, although how they interpret that feeling is related to the environment in which they find themselves. In fact they suggested that emotions were simply the interpretation of changes in physiology, although it was later concluded that emotions were actually an interaction between physiological responses and perception. However, we must not downplay the effects of chemicals, be they self-produced in the way of neurotransmitters, or synthetically by way of pills.

Figure 2.11 *The hippy culture of the 1960s was associated with drug-taking and led to the Peace and Love movement*

There is considerable and irrefutable evidence that drugs can severely change the behaviour of the person concerned. We are all aware of the effects of 'recreational drugs' such as ecstasy, LSD and amphetamines, which work by altering brain chemistry. Drugs can also alter behaviours in a therapeutic way. For example, schizophrenia, if left untreated, can result in the most bizarre behaviours and acute distress. However, when given anti-psychotic drugs, most schizophrenics can live relatively normal lives. This indicates that our biochemistry – part of our physiology – must have a huge influence on our subsequent behaviours. Depressives have been found to have low levels of the neurotransmitter serotonin, and this seems to change how they feel about the world, reducing their desire to interact with others or become involved in normal everyday events. When we analyse human behaviour, we should never dismiss the effects of our brain chemistry on the way that we feel.

Physical appearance

One area of biopsychology deals with physical appearance. It makes sense to think that how we behave bears some relationship to our appearance. In a physically demanding – or threatening – situation, a male who is six foot tall, muscular and fit is a lot less likely to feel intimidated than a female who is only five foot tall and a real wuss! Also, people who believe they are attractive often behave in a different way from people who perceive themselves to be ugly. The former are generally more confident and outgoing. Recently, there was a newspaper article about a young woman who suffered from body dysmorphic disorder, a condition in which sufferers are preoccupied with an imagined defect in their appearance. This young woman's life was severely affected by her belief that she was ugly and ungainly, to the extent that she would not leave the house.

Early theories of personality linked appearance to subsequent behaviour. One such theory, phrenology, proposed by Gall in the early nineteenth century, was based on the idea that 37 specific areas of the brain were responsible for different abilities or behaviours. Consequently the size of a specific area of the head, be it large or small, would dictate the subsequent behaviour of the person. Somatotype theory also emerged about a century later, focusing on body shape. Kretschmer (1925) argued that certain mental illnesses related to body shape, such as the connection between schizophrenia and thin, fragile types of people. I suppose he forgot to take into account that schizophrenics are often very distressed, lose their appetites and therefore become thin and fragile. He also suggested that people who were more rounded were more likely to suffer from manic depression (bipolar disorder)! Another theory proposed by Sheldon in (1954) correlated personality and body shape. This is discussed in relation to age and appearance in the individual differences section (page 46).

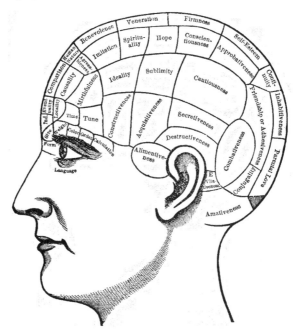

Figure 2.12 *A phrenological head*

Circadian rhythms

Each one of us has a biological clock and this influences our behaviour, level of arousal and ability to function. The twenty-four-hour cycle of the normal adult day, the monthly cycle of women and the annual cycle (which may well influence such disorders as seasonal affective disorder) all influence our behaviour. Although we are not certain about the function of sleep despite copious research, we do know that without it we don't function as well as if we have a good eight hours a night. Dement and Kleitman (1957) demonstrated how sleep cycles work and further research has shown that if we are deprived of REM sleep, our cognitive functioning declines considerably. The time of year (SAD), the time of the month (premenstrual tension or PMT) or the time of day (tiredness or change in body temperature) can all have an impact on subsequent behaviours.

Some key concepts of biopsychology
- All behaviour is purely a result of the biological functioning of the body or biochemical changes in the brain.
- Any illness or maladaptive behaviour is a result of a structural defect or the physiological malfunctioning.
- Over-arousal/stress can often explain changes in behaviour.
- Reductionism often uses the ideas of biopsychology in reducing all behaviour to its most basic components.
- Our perception of physical appearance can affect our behaviour.
- Behaviours can be species-specific or common to all animals (e.g. the fight or flight mechanism).
- Genetics can be used to explain the continuation of behaviours from one generation to the next.
- Emotions are no more than the interpretation of our physical response to a stimulus.
- Drugs can severely alter behaviour and change our perceptions, emotions and behaviour.
- We have circadian rhythms and patterns of sleep which, if disrupted, can lead to a decrement in performance.

Therefore in order to explain behaviour in terms of biopsychological theories, apply the questions shown in Figure 2.13 to the study.

THE PERSPECTIVE OF INDIVIDUAL DIFFERENCES ••••

The final perspective we are going to consider is the perspective that seeks to identify and measure the differences between one person and another. This is usually done by comparing people to what are known as group norms. Group norms are in fact the average scores or measurements for a group of people, which are taken to be the 'normal' scores for that group. Therefore if we compare a person's score with the group

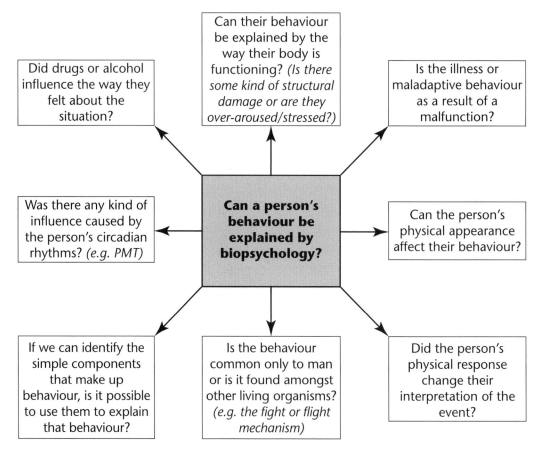

Figure 2.13

norm, we get an idea of how similar or how different they are to an average member of their group.

The problem is that everyone is actually very different and the process of trying to put them into categories is unnatural and often masks the real causes of behaviour. After all, we may all behave in the same way, but our reasons for that behaviour could be extremely diverse. We should therefore not simply look at the categories of behaviour but look at the motivation behind that behaviour. If we take this into account, especially when we consider the numerous theories and models which have been suggested to make sense of human behaviour, it makes it much easier to understand that not everyone will behave in a predicted way. In fact, looking at individual differences is important when evaluating models or theories that do not take into account idiosyncratic variation between individuals.

This approach is called the **idiographic** approach, and is in sharp contrast to the **nomothetic** approach, which suggests that we can accurately quantify people in terms of scores or categories. There are a number of nomothetic theorists such as

Hans Eysenck, who believe that we can score people on universal traits such as the personality traits of extroversion/introversion and neuroticism/stability. Although such traits exist, the minute you give people a score or label, they will start to compare themselves with others, which gives rise to ethical questions. Should we categorise people? There will always be people on the fringes of the categories and they might then see themselves as abnormal, or worse still, may be categorised as abnormal by the rest of society.

Individual differences as a form of survival

If you accept the idea of evolution, then it should make sense to see the individual differences between people as fundamentally important. Individuals differ genetically, and these differences can give them a reproductive advantage over other individuals. In fact Darwin pointed out that there are numerous examples of ways in which animals have adapted in order to survive, for example, by growing longer or shorter beaks, or by developing less or more hair depending on the climate. Humans are the most advanced animal species, but we have still had to adapt to cope with our environment. Recent research has shown that we share a limited number of common ancestors and yet there is a huge amount of diversity between members of the human race. This indicates that as we have developed, we have adapted to the various environments we inhabit. Perhaps the most obvious example of this relates to skin colour. To survive in an environment where the sun is at its hottest (around the equator) without developing sun-burn and ultimately skin cancers, we need to produce large levels of skin pigmentation. Dark skin is therefore a characteristic of people whose ancestors originate from very hot environments.

Figure 2.14 *These dark-skinned people are more resistant to damage from the sun's rays*

So why isn't all behaviour an adaptation to the environment? Much of it is, and this can be seen from the adaptations that characterise different species through to individual adaptations. Species adaptations involve all members of the species, and allow the species to survive and reproduce in the environment in which they live. A personal adaptation allows the individual to develop more subtle defence mechanisms to help them survive in a hostile environment. Therefore when we try to understand people's behaviour, it is essential to keep in mind that their behaviour in certain situations is merely a survival mechanism and should be explained as such.

Cultural differences

We have already discussed cultural differences in perception and learning experiences. There are also social influences which may explain the behaviour of the individuals from a particular society. Take, for example, family size. Some cultures have much larger families than the average western family although this often seems to coincide with a much higher mortality rate amongst young children. In some other cultures, male children are rated as more 'valuable'; for example, in China they are seen as potential earners (and financial providers for their parents' old age) and so are more enthusiastically supported, educated, and consequently have higher self-esteem. Other cultures have also valued male children over female children such as the Eskimo culture, where conditions of life have been so severe that, in the past, the practice of killing female children shortly after birth would ensure that they were not left for the family to support in case of lack of potential husbands.

I have been surprised at the differences even between closely related cultures, such as the English and North Americans. We take for granted that many of the famous past studies in psychology have been conducted in North America, and sometimes accept that although they are American participants, the results can be applied universally. However, many aspects of American life are totally different to our own in the UK. First of all, the USA is like a collection of different countries with different norms and values within the same landmass. Walking doesn't seem to be a pastime that many people engage in, and many of the building designs are based on easy vehicular accessibility, for example to the huge shopping malls or eating emporiums. Many American states don't tolerate teenage drinking or smoking at all, which seems to result in some American teenagers remaining 'younger' for longer than our own. There are also many areas in the US where small communities thrive, and there is a greater emphasis on religion than in many areas of the UK. I would also say that on the whole, Americans are far less racist, ageist and weightist than the British (despite what you might expect from media images – see Figure 2.15).

We also have to bear in mind the fact that many of the different cultural groups have a much higher self-image than thirty years ago (Hraba and Grant, 1970) and

Figure 2.15 Familiar for the US – strange for the UK?

this in itself could explain the chosen difference in behaviours of people from different racial groups.

Personality

None of us would dispute that there are different 'types' of people, from the avid party-goer to the quiet loner, the worrier to the laid-back dude who never seems to get concerned about anything. These differences in behaviour are influenced, according to personality theorists, by the personality of the individuals. Personality can be considered 'a distinctive and relatively stable pattern of behaviours, thought, motives and emotions that characterise an individual' (Banyard and Hayes,1994, p58). This implies that we will behave in a similar way in different situations, although we all know that we can change in different situations and even over time. We may feel confident with our friends, but if we are in a situation where we know no one, we may become quiet and reserved. Similarly, as we get older, we often become less reckless or 'laddish' than when we are younger.

Personality theorists would argue that different personality types are identifiable, (although the actual types will depend on the beliefs of the theorist). However, there are recurrent findings that personality seems to be measurable on five different scales, known as robust factors – extroversion, emotional stability, agreeableness, control and culture.

Extroversion: the degree to which we are outgoing and enjoy the company of others. The other end of the scale is known as introversion.
Emotional stability: how laid-back we are, or conversely, how prone we are to getting worried, anxious or neurotic.
Agreeableness: how friendly and generous we are.
Control: how controlled, organised and self-disciplined we are.
Culture: this category includes traits such as curiosity, creativity, knowledge and intelligence.

The same theorists are also likely to claim that the type to which we belong will probably influence our behaviour in a research situation; for example, a confident extrovert may fare more favourably on some tests which involve interaction with others, whilst a nervous introvert may appear to fare far worse. However, if you could take these factors into account and sort out some way of balancing them, they would probably perform equally well. There is also the argument that birth position influences assertiveness and confidence, with older children in a family sometimes being more confident than younger children and the youngest being the most assertive. This should also be taken into account when quantifying behaviours.

Appearance and age

There is a large body of research which suggests that our appearance has a huge influence on how we are treated by others. One of the early pieces of research I mentioned earlier in the last section relates to the influence of appearance on other people and was conducted by Sheldon (1954) after he examined thousands of photographs of different people. He concluded that there were three main body shapes – the endomorph (who is rounded and sometimes overweight), the ectomorph (who is thin and scrawny with little muscle) and the mesomorph (who is muscular and athletic). (See Figure 2.16 on page 47.)

Research undertaken by Ryckman (1989) involved asking subjects to rate pictures of male and female versions of each of these three body types on a range of expected personality characteristics. The endomorphs were seen as less attractive and less healthy, although the female endomorphs were seen as neater and cleaner than the males. Ectomorphs were seen as intelligent and neat and more socially popular than endomorphs, and the mesomorphs were seen as more hard-working and better looking than the other groups (although the males were perceived as less intelligent and sloppier than the females). If this is the case, how might these different body shapes influence the way that their owners are treated?

Western culture sets great store by physical appearance. Ask any group of women in this country whether they are currently dieting and you are likely to get a high

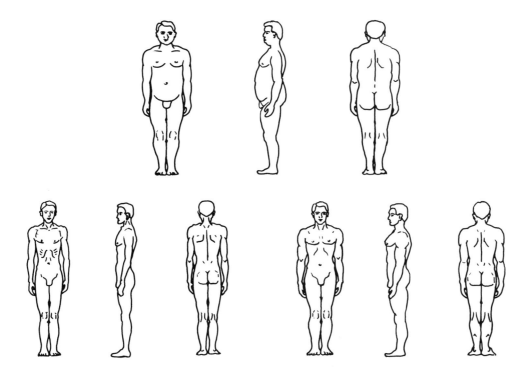

Figure 2.16 *The endomorph (top), ectomorph (left) and mesomorph body types (right)*

percentage of positive responses. In fact a group of students undertook a study for their coursework fairly recently asking women and men to rate their current body size, their ideal body size and what they thought would be the most attractive body size to the opposite sex. This was partially replicating the work of Fallon and Rozin (1985) who discovered that many female college students were dissatisfied with their weight and saw themselves as overweight and therefore unattractive to men, whereas the men preferred bodies that were considerably heavier than the women had estimated (see Figure 2.17 on page 48). The other interesting finding of the Fallon and Rozin study was that the men's ratings of their current size, ideal size and the features that they thought women would find attractive were very similar, whereas there was a large difference between the women's three ratings.

If women feel so insecure about their appearance, is this not going to have an effect on their self-esteem and result in a lack of confidence? Despite attempts to present larger figures as acceptable (for example, the supermodel Sophie Dahl), the majority of women, given the opportunity, would, I am sure, opt to be slim and lithe. Look at the way certain members of the Spice Girls have become thin almost overnight!

Similarly, if we were a scrawny, short and weak-looking male, we would probably not have as much confidence as we would if we were six feet tall, muscular and

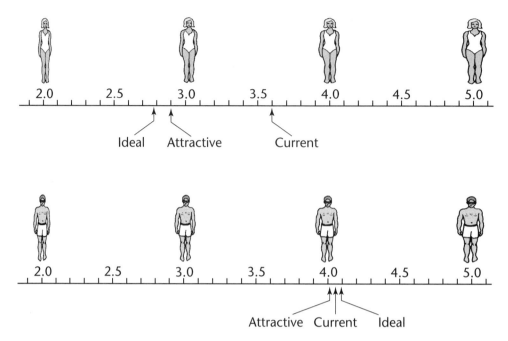

Figure 2.17 *Men and women's perceptions of their own weight, according to Fallon and Rozin (1985)*

athletic. Evidence has shown that taller men are chosen for jobs more often than similarly qualified but shorter men, and that taller graduates receive higher starting salaries than shorter graduates (Feldman, 1971). Research by Wilson (1968) discovered that different groups of students perceived the same man to be a different height depending on the status he was given when he was introduced to them. In fact his estimated height increased by five inches from when he was introduced in the first instance as a student, then as a member of other occupational categories, until finally as a professor. This suggests that taller men are perceived as more competent.

Finally the factor of age may well influence not only the behaviour of the person, but the responses they get from others. We all know that there are times when younger people feel they are not taken seriously by the older generations, and older people feel that they have lost their status and credibility in the eyes of the young. How many times do you see these stereotypical roles portrayed on television, with the young being seen as arrogant and self-centred (Harry Enfield's Kevin the teenager) or the elderly being tolerated and by-passed by their younger relatives? These stereotypical images can influence the behaviour of the groups themselves and affect the way that our society treats them.

It is extremely likely that the factors relating to appearance and age discussed above influence the experiences and opportunities we have in our lives. In fact, there is considerable evidence to show that attractive people are treated with more leniency and given more opportunities than ugly people. Age also makes a difference because, on the whole, the older we get, the less adventurous we become and the more cautious, more often than not because we are more aware of the potential dangers. None of us are identical, and so the differences between us are bound to have some effect on whether we are confident or shy, successful or a failure.

Abnormality

Another area where we, as individuals, show considerable variation is our behaviour on a day-to-day basis. Take, for example, the situation where a person bumps into you in a pub; you may respond angrily and threaten to punch the person, or you may simply ignore the collision and carry on talking to your friends. Neither response is actually abnormal (although the first may be a little extreme); however, there are acceptable limits for these different behaviours and the limits seem to be dictated by the society in which we live. If we exceed the limits set (flattening the man, *and* jumping up and down on him), we may well be seen as 'abnormal', although the response may really have been understandable if past events were taken into account (the person had previously hit your car, stolen your girlfriend and lost you your job).

Bearing these factors in mind, it makes sense to see how erroneous it is to suggest that we will all behave in similar ways. However, demonstrations of unusual behaviour over time may well be labelled as 'abnormal' or mentally ill.

I think very few people would dispute the need to have some kind of diagnostic tool for deciding who is suffering from a 'psychiatric disorder', not least because the process of categorising people makes it easier to decide the required treatments to alleviate their suffering or discomfort, or even the danger they pose to themselves and possibly to others. However, the problem is that these categorisations can be inaccurate. Not only do we all exhibit some kind of 'weird' behaviour from time to time (due, for example, to being over-tired, stressed or under the influence of alcohol), but we may exhibit different 'weird' behaviours depending on the situation. However this doesn't automatically mean that we have some kind of psychiatric illness.

A further problem with the definition of psychiatric illnesses is that what is considered abnormal in one culture may not be in another. Even qualified practitioners within our own culture have a problem. Rosenhan (1973), for example, discovered that psychiatrists were unable to differentiate between the sane and the insane in psychiatric hospitals. If they were unable to categorise people accurately using the Diagnostic and Statistical Manual of the American Psychiatric Association (the DSM), considered a reliable and valuable tool, this in itself is a problem. Also, diagnoses for the same problem may differ, even between western cultures, according to the person making the diagnosis and the person being diagnosed. However, by labelling people (rightly or wrongly), we can influence the way that they are treated, maybe for the rest of their lives. If we consider individual differences, the behaviour of people who are categorised as psychiatrically disordered may seem far less 'abnormal'. After all, multiple personality disorder (now known as dissociative identity disorder) is recognised as a psychiatric disorder, and yet it has also been explained as being a kind of coping mechanism.

Psychometric testing

I mentioned earlier that the minute you put a numerical value on a person, they will be compared to others, a practice which upsets some psychologists who believe it is unfair to make comparisons as we are all individuals. This process is actually a major part of the 'psychology industry' within the field of occupational psychology and has a multi-million pound turnover. Here, potential candidates sit batteries of tests to assess their effectiveness in different situations.

However, in order for this whole process to be effective, the tests themselves must be reliable, valid and have standardised scores. What happens if the tests being used to compare people are not relevant or fair, due to say, cultural bias? Gould's (1982) article showed how dangerous it was to try and categorise people with tests that are inappropriate. This whole concept can be used to discriminate or define ways of dealing with categorised people that are equally unfair. No doubt in some point in your life, you have sat some kind of written test in which you did not do as well as you felt you should have. The reason for this may well have been because you were over-aroused, or that you were tired. Imagine, now, that this was going to affect the way that you were to be treated forever. We must therefore take into account, when people perform any kind of psychometric test, whether it is appropriate for them, and ensure that they are not so stressed out about the test that they produce false results.

Some of key concepts of 'individual difference' theories
- We are all unique and therefore the only way that we can consider a person's behaviour is to look at them as an individual.
- The self-image of different racial groups has improved over the past thirty years and this may explain the maintained diversity of different cultures.
- Is the personality of the person a result of life experiences? If this is the case we must interpret their behaviour accordingly.
- Differences in appearance, e.g. age, attractiveness and gender, can affect behaviour.
- No one can be regarded as abnormal as we are unable to define and diagnose abnormality accurately.
- Psychometric testing should be regarded with caution, as it is very easy to label different groups by giving them inappropriate tests.

A very brief summary of how we can explain research using different perspectives

One of the topics which gives us a good example of how to use different perspectives for explaining behaviour is to consider the subject of smoking.

There are a number of possible ways of explaining the 'behaviour' of smoking according to the different perspectives. I have here used simple explanations as an illustration. You will also notice that many of the explanations are interlinked.

Cognitive explanations

The cognitive explanation would consider the thought processes and reasoning which may have resulted in the smoker's behaviour. Research by Barton *et al.* (1982) and McKennell and Bynner (1969) found that both males and females between the ages of 11 and 15 associate smoking with looking tough rather than timid, and being attractive and sexually aware. This association will have come from some kind of learning whereby images of smokers were portrayed in ways which reinforced these beliefs. The young people made a fundamental attribution error that it was the smoking rather than the person that caused the effect. This in turn would influence the memory and thoughts of the adolescent and may well become part of a 'grown-up' schema. The idea that smoking helps with weight control may have influenced some of the girls (and is supported by the preoccupation with weight and body image today).

Child developmental theories

The smoker may have been influenced by a more powerful role model to smoke; that is, they learned by observation and imitated the behaviour. This links in with the cognitive theory of learning affecting thinking. It might also be possible to explain smoking behaviour in terms of Freudian theory, with the suggestion that the child has become orally fixated during their development, and thus finds the need to satiate its oral desires by constantly puffing on cigarettes.

Social theories

Smoking usually starts when people reach their teens. Severson and Lichtenstein (1986) found that adolescents are more likely to smoke if their parents and friends smoke. This would indicate that they are possibly imitating adult role models (their parents) and Leventhal *et al.* (1985) also suggested that smokers generally smoke their first cigarettes in the company of peers who encourage them, suggesting that there may be some element of conforming to group norms.

Biological explanations

Biological explanations would look at the physical effects of smoking on the body. Ovide and Pomerlea (1989) suggest that people come to depend on the effects of nicotine, the addictive chemical in cigarettes. Nicotine triggers a chain reaction in the body which results in an increase in arousal, concentration, memory and alertness and also feelings of pleasure. This response, caused by the nicotine in the bloodstream, decays after between 20–60 minutes, triggering the desire to have another cigarette to maintain that level of arousal. To support this idea, Schachter *et al.* (1977) showed that smokers who smoked low-nicotine cigarettes smoked on average more than when they were smoking high-nicotine cigarettes. This idea that the maintenance of this level is of primary importance to smokers explains why they find it so hard to give up; they have come to rely on nicotine as a coping mechanism.

Individual differences

Here we would have to look at the people concerned. We would need to consider background, physique, age, gender and cultural norms. We would take into account that people start smoking for different reasons, rather than expecting one theory to be an adequate explanation of all instances.

Therefore in order to explain behaviour in terms of theories of individual difference, apply the questions given in Figure 2.18.

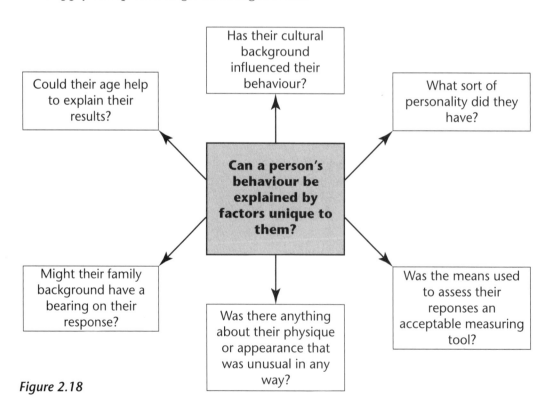

Figure 2.18

The nature–nurture debate

3

> **Introduction to the Human Genome Project and how it is now taking over from the original nature–nurture debate.**

I am sure that you will have heard about the **Human Genome Project** which started in 1990. It is a 13-year effort which has been coordinated in the USA by the Department of Energy and the National Institute of Health. It is an attempt to completely map the entire spectrum of genetic materials found in all humans. All humans have genomes – a genome is all the DNA in an organism – which contains the complete set of genetic instructions (genes) on the 23 pairs of chromosomes that we all have. These genes carry the information necessary for making the proteins required by organisms. They may determine, among other things, how the person looks (although identical twins often look less alike as they age), how well their metabolism works, how good the person is at resisting infection or illness and sometimes how they behave.

One of the goals of the Human Genome Project is to discover the functions of specific genes and find out what happens if they don't work. This will greatly assist in the development of new ways to diagnose and treat human disorders and will help to prevent them occurring by targeting the causes. Another aspect of genetic research is genetic modification – an area that has provoked huge controversy in crop research. The idea of producing disease-resistant crops with higher yields is appealing when we

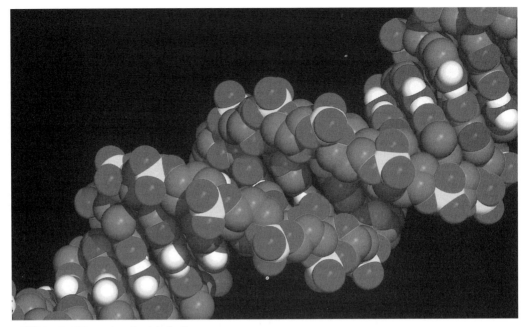

Figure 3.1 *The DNA double helix*

consider the amount of famine in less developed countries, but people's resistance stems from their concerns about interfering with nature and its possible repercussions. Take this argument further, and consider the potential ethical problems with human genetic modification.

To give you some idea of the complexity of a human genome, let me briefly explain the structure of DNA. The DNA molecules that carry our genetic instructions are made up of four simple bases (or building blocks) – adenine, cytosine, guanine and thymine. They pair up to form the DNA double helix (see Figure 3.1). Each one of our cells contains about six billion base pairs of DNA (three billion from each parent), however it seems that the differences between us are actually fairly small. In fact it has been estimated that only one base pair in every thousand accounts for the differences between us – we have far more in common with each other than was originally thought. However, it is these differences which determine our genetic predisposition to things such as disease resistance or behaviour. Interestingly, the project is also looking at a number of non-human organisms too, such as the human gut bacterium *Escherichia coli*, the fruit fly and the laboratory mouse. The surprising thing is that we share many similarities in our DNA with other species too.

So why are we, as psychologists, interested in the Human Genome Project? The main reason is it may tell us to what extent our personality, interests and behaviour can be traced back to our biology – can someone really be born' bad' or 'clever'? Even more interesting, but still in the realms of sci-fi at the present time, is whether we could manipulate or manufacture genes to create the perfect human being. Does this remind you of the eugenics movement by any chance? More about eugenics in the next section.

THE HISTORY OF GENETICS ● ● ● ● ● ● ● ● ● ● ● ● ● ● ● ● ●

Psychologists have always been interested in the inheritance of family characteristics and how they account for biological variations, however the term 'genetics' did not appear in scientific research until 1909. Sir Francis Galton (1822–1911) is credited with being the first scientist to systematically study heredity and human behaviour. Galton was the cousin of Charles Darwin, so not surprisingly he believed in the idea of inheritance and studied correlations between relatives to learn what characteristics might be inherited. At the same time, American scientists such as Charles B. Davenport were using the ideas of Gregor J. Mendel (known as Mendelian concepts) to show how pauperism, feeblemindedness, manic depression, criminality, shiftlessness and other unwanted traits could be passed from one generation to the next. Using research with animals they suggested ways of getting rid of these unwanted traits by restricting and controlling human reproduction.

In the late nineteenth century, Galton christened the movement which had as its foundation the belief that social traits are inherited – the Eugenics Movement (eugenics means 'well-born'). Research conducted into the idea of eugenics involved looking for family patterns in alcoholism, criminality and insanity. Making huge inferences, certain behaviours were attributed to different races. Davenport, for example, believed that Italians were more likely to commit crimes of violence, Greeks were more likely to be slovenly and the Swedes were a tidy race! As a result of these conjectures, it was thought that the problems of society could be sorted out by addressing the root cause – prevent the reproduction of 'inferior' peoples and you have solved the problems! By 1935, thirty states in the USA had passed sterilisation laws to prevent certain reproductive behaviours and other countries followed suit. Nazi Germany, as we know, carried out mass sterilisation and then extermination, and Alberta in Canada continued involuntary sterilisations of 'inferiors' until 1971 and Alabama in the USA continued until 1973. In fact in 1985, nineteen states in the USA still had laws which allowed the sterilisation of people with mental disabilities.

THE EARLY INVESTIGATION OF HEREDITY ● ● ● ● ● ● ● ● ●

We have already mentioned the early studies with animals as a way of looking at inheritance. The way that heredity was originally investigated was by observing similarities between family members, but it was impossible to distinguish the effects of inheritance from those of the environment. Following on, researchers turned to twin and adoptive studies as far back as seventy years ago. Probably one of the most famous ongoing studies is the research headed by Thomas Bouchard at the University of Minnesota Centre for Twin and Adoption Research.

Twin studies use both identical and fraternal twins – the first are genetically identical as they come from the same fertilised egg which splits in two (monozygotic twins – Mz). Fraternal twins develop from separate eggs which are fertilised by two different sperm (dizygotic twins – Dz). Therefore any traits shared by Mz twins are likely to have been inherited. However, it is probable that Mz twins will have been brought up in very similar ways within the same environment, and this could result in genetic influences being confused wth environmental ones.

The solution is to look at identical twins who have been reared apart, but this situation is rare. Often they are brought up in similar (if not the same) environment – simply by different family members, or else the adoption agencies responsible for placing the identical twins try to find them families with circumstances similar to their original one in terms of economic status, religion and cultural interests.

Figure 3.2 *Identical twins provide a way of researching the influence of heredity on our behaviour*

So far twin-study specialists have concluded that genes account for between 40 and 60 per cent of the variation in human psychological traits. But we need to take into account that twins studies probably don't represent the population as a whole because generally the participants are volunteers. There is also the confounding factor of appearance, for example twins who are very tall are likely to both score high on extroversion and self-confidence because past research has indicated that tall people are often treated with more respect and given more attention than shorter people. However, there are other types of adoption studies that provide evidence of inherited characteristics that involve looking at twins who weren't placed in similar homes and yet still display similar traits and behaviours.

There is an ongoing study, the **Minnesota Study of Twins Reared Apart**, which addresses this question. In 1990, there were over 56 pairs of twins who fitted the required category. These sets of twins were separated, on average, at ten weeks of age and raised in different environments for an average of 34 years. They were compared with a group of identical twins raised together to see if the ones reared apart were as similar to each other as the ones reared together, and the correlations between the two sets of twins for personality characteristics were almost identical (0.49 for identical twins reared apart, and 0.52 for identical twins reared together). They were also compared to fraternal twins raised apart and together and it was found that these sets of twins had far lower correlations (0.21 and 0.23 respectively). The findings were taken to indicate that genes play a greater part in personality development than environmental experiences.

One of the findings from the study which indicated these shared genetic characteristics came from a pair of twins with strikingly different backgrounds. Oskar Stohr and Jack Yufe were born in Trinidad. They had a Jewish father and German mother who parted soon after their birth. The father raised Jack as a Jew, and Jack spent part of his childhood on an Israeli kibbutz. In stark contrast, Oskar was taken to Germany by his mother and raised by his grandmother as a Catholic Nazi. Throughout their lives, they had no contact with each other apart from one meeting when they were in their late twenties. They took part in the Minnesota study when they were in their late forties and amazed the researchers by the similarities between them. They both arrived wearing the same clothes, and looking very similar with moustaches and wire-rimmed glasses. They had similar (if somewhat strange) mannerisms and personalities and shared a number of likes and dislikes which neither knew about. Because they had been separated so early in their lives, it is unlikely that these mannerisms could have been learned, indicating that there must have been some kind of genetic component.

Despite this interest in heredity and the desire to identify genes for specific behaviours we must also remember that it is unlikely that any 'pure' behaviour could be passed on. Each of us has a different set of life experiences which might modify the genetic input and perhaps even cancel it out altogether. More specific studies of genetic influences on human behaviour are now emerging as a result of the development of DNA-based techniques.

The Human Genome Project came about from work undertaken by the Department of Energy in the USA, which was trying to detect any changes in the genetic materials of people who had been affected by radiation. As these technologies for working with DNA developed during the 1980s, the idea arose to systematically sequence the entire human genome. Once this was done, it would never have to be repeated. The project really began in 1988 when the Department of Energy and the National Institute of Health signed a Memorandum which committed them to work together, although the project wasn't publicly launched until 1st October, 1990.

IS THERE A GENE THAT RELATES TO EVERY KIND OF BEHAVIOUR? ●

Despite the geneticists' efforts, the genes that interest psychologists such as those which relate to nurturing, intelligence, personality, aggression or sexual preference have still not been identified, if indeed they ever will. Perhaps our definitions of the traits we are interested in are part of the problem. Take, for example, intelligence and consider for a moment what we actually mean by intelligence. We have no universally accepted definition for intelligence. In fact, trying to find such a definition is one of the enduring problems that face psychologists, and yet here we are trying to find a gene for it! Robert Plomin is probably one of the most well-known researchers involved in hunting for an 'intelligence gene'. But even after extensive research it seems that there isn't an identifiable 'intelligence gene' after all. Even Plomin (1990) has stated that although 30 per cent of individual differences in intelligence among children are due to heredity, the percentage goes up as the child's age increases. He suggests that by adulthood the similarities between children and their blood relations is nearer to 50 per cent, but we must remember that environmental and lifestyle differences are greater between parents and their younger children than they are when those children become adults. This indicates that intelligence – whatever it is – also has some environmental input.

If we are not sure what we mean by intelligence, then perhaps we should take another look at what we are looking for. I personally think that intelligence is a whole collection of skills, one of which is the ability to learn. Perhaps, rather than looking for an overall concept which we call 'intelligence', we should try to look for more specific skills. If this is acceptable, it makes more sense to look at the work of a molecular biologist who works at Princeton University in the USA.

Interestingly enough, mice are a convenient medium to investigate the genetic roots of behaviour. They are readily available, have a fast rate of breeding and it is easy to control their environment. Even more importantly, the mouse genome is very similar to ours, apparently having the same components but arranged in a different order. Scientists have discovered ways of modifying the genes of mice, for example inactivating certain genes, and thereby studying the resulting behaviour.

In the late summer of 1999 the results of such research, undertaken by Joe Tsien into the genetic influence on learning ability, were published. These results indicated that it was possible to improve the ability of mice to learn by genetically modifying a gene, which allowed them to make more than the usual amount of a subunit of a certain protein called the N-methyl-D-aspartate (NMDA) receptor. NMDA receptors help to strengthen the connection between two neurones and these connections are the basis for learning and memory.

Figure 3.3

The mice that had had these genetic modifications were known as 'Doogie' mice (after the American TV programme **about** a child genius called Doogie Howser MD). These Doogie mice were compared **with** a control group on a number of basic learning tests such as distinguishing between objects or remembering how to find a platform in a tank of coloured water. It was found that the experimental group performed significantly better than the control group. Consequently the news reached the media who claimed immediately that Tsien had discovered the 'IQ gene' or 'smart gene' but as you and I know, memory is only a part of intelligence. However, he had discovered one genetic aspect of mental capacity and at least it is a start. It also has implications for trying to correct the problems caused by such illnesses as Alzheimer's disease or even to combat the problems associated with strokes, but as yet there is still more research to be done.

Further research with mice has indicated that some strains of mice are extremely aggressive, and some crave alcohol. These findings have been linked to very low levels of neurotransmitters which may well have a genetic basis. The next step is to identify the gene responsible and then look for its counterpart in humans and see whether it has a similar effect. The problem comes with trying to distinguish the behavioural element from the numerous other confounding variables.

'Mice that appeared predisposed to addiction because they kept returning to a morphine-laced drinking bottle, for example, turned out instead to hate the quinine spiking the alternate choice. Is a rodent that strikes at another mouse on top of its cage more

aggressive? Or it is more anxious, claustrophobic or sensitive to shadow? To add to the confusion, what looks like a measurable behaviour could be the side effect of a physical characteristic. A mouse that seems to be aggressive say, might have an unusually low physical pain threshold – and so is hurting, grumpy and prone to strike others.'

Sally Lehrman (1998)

More recently the field of human behavioural genetics has sought to understand that there are both genetic and environmental influences on people's behaviour – the ultimate nature–nurture debate. One branch of behavioural genetics is that of behavioural genetic determinism – the belief that genetics is the major factor in determining behaviour. However, having looked at summaries of some of the key areas of genetic behavioural research in humans, every one of them involves some kind of controversy or counter claim.

In 1990, psychiatrist Ernest Noble of UCLA and pharmacologist Kenneth Blum of the University of Texas in San Antonio, who had been researching **alcoholism**, reported a strong association between one version of a gene and alcoholism. They found this particular gene in more than two-thirds of 35 deceased alcoholics, compared to one-fifth of the same number of non-alcoholics. Their research had involved family studies that indicated an inherited tendency to drink excessively. However, six months later, a team at the National Institute of Alcohol Abuse and Alcoholism disputed their findings, saying they were unable to find any genetic difference between the two groups. Despite four more pieces of contradictory evidence, Blum and Noble stuck with their findings and eventually research by a medical geneticist, David Comings of the City of Hope Medical Centre in Duarte, California, supported their

Figure 3.4 *How much of a role do genes play in this (stereotypical) alcoholic's behaviour?*

original hypothesis. The gene has been called a 'reward' gene which is associated with other kinds of compulsive disorders besides alcoholism such as cocaine addiction and obesity.

The '**Gay Gene**' was 'discovered' in 1994 by LeVay and Hamer who announced that they had found a section of the X-chromosome shared by gay brothers. The problem was that the research design was weak. The team had looked at the X-chromosomes of 40 pairs of gay brothers who had been a self-selecting sample gathered from advertisements in gay magazines. They found that 82 per cent shared genetic markers in one region and so he concluded that men who had inherited these markers were predisposed to becoming gay. The problem was that they failed to look at the chromosomes of any of the men's 'straight' brothers. If they had found that these brothers also shared the same genetic markers, this would have made the findings less significant.

There has been no other support for the idea of a 'gay gene', although Hamer undertook further research using another sample of 33 pairs of gay brothers. In this research he found that about 66 per cent shared the same genetic markers. Hamer also looked at heterosexual brothers and lesbian sisters who came from the same families but here he found no association with the marker. Further work by Michael Bailey of Northwestern University and Richard C. Pillard of Boston University found that in 52 per cent of the identical twins they surveyed, both men were gay. They also discovered that 22 per cent of the fraternal twins were also gay, both of which indicate a genetic link somewhere along the line. However, male siblings (who actually share the same amount of genes as Dz twins) showed only a nine per cent concordance level. So, is homosexuality inherited? We still cannot be sure.

Hamer did not stop with gay genes. In November 1996, he was part of a group that suggested that mood was influenced by a specific gene. One mutation appeared to induce self-confidence and good cheer while another seemed to predispose people to chronic anxiety. This gene seems to regulate serotonin (the 'feel good' neurotransmitter) and Hamer also suggested that the gene may also be linked to alcoholism and smoking. Watch this space!

With regard to a gene for a predisposition to violence, we are even further from establishing concrete evidence. Most of the research undertaken on humans has, so far, had flaws in design, and provoked tremendous ethical controversy. For example in April 1998 a report was issued about research carried out on boys from low income families who were believed to have violent inherited tendencies. However, not all the boys had been in trouble. In fact the sample included 100 African American and Latino boys who were chosen only because their older brothers had been in trouble with the law. Sally Lehrman (1998) described how researchers in New York administered the now-recalled diet drug fenfluramine to the boys in the hope that they would be able to find out whether the drug, which triggers the brain to release serotonin, could lessen aggression. The study was so seriously flawed that the results were ignored – not only was it unethical but some of the boys had already been treated for attention-deficit disorder.

Then in August 1998 the Massachusetts state senator James Jajuga suggested that DNA collected from parolees could be used to help to develop a 'criminal' genetic profile. The idea was that this would help law enforcement officers to prevent re-offending through education, drug therapy or counselling. The ethical issues surrounding such research don't need an explanation; are the parolees giving their informed consent – what will happen to the data they provide?

Whether it will be possible to ultimately map specific behaviours to individual genes remains to be seen. McInerney (1999) suggests that 'behaviours, like all complex traits, involve *multiple genes*, a reality that complicates the search for genetic contributions.' He goes on to explain that in order to look at the relationships between genes and behaviour, we have to study both families and populations in order to compare the behaviours of those who have the genes in question and those who do not. The trouble is, this usually results in nothing more than some kind of statistical construct that estimates the amount of variation in a population we can attribute to genetic factors. As you know, the results will only relate to the population under consideration. If the population were different or if the research were undertaken in a different environment, it is quite likely that the level of heredity will change as well.

THE ETHICAL IMPLICATIONS OF GENETIC RESEARCH

Are our behaviours inbred? Are they 'written indelibly in our genes as immutable biological imperatives, or is the environment more important in shaping our thoughts and actions?' (McInerney and Rothstein, 2001). How will we ever know? Without answers to these questions, we are left in a situation which is fraught with ethical problems.

James Watson won the Nobel Prize in Physiology in Medicine in 1962 for co-discovering the structure of DNA. He recognised that knowledge gained from studies like the Human Genome Project have tremendous medical and societal implications. As a result, alongside the progress of the Genome Project, there has also been a programme established to look at the ethical, legal and social implications of genome research. How well they manage to control the information gained by the research is another matter.

If you remember the influence of such work as the intelligence testing of Yerkes at the beginning of the First World War, you will realise what implications genetic research may well have. For example, how would we use the genetic information fairly? Could we use it to discriminate between individuals? What about the necessity of genetic counselling and the influence of genetic factors on medical practice;

how would knowledge of genetic factors influence personal reproductive decisions and might there be a 'cost' for ignoring genetic guidelines? An example of this would be if a woman was told she was carrying a child who has an increased likelihood of developing a disease such as breast cancer. Would this be sufficient to make her choose to abort the foetus, knowing the potential effects of treatment such as radiotherapy or mastectomy and that it may, in any case, not be effective? What about the likelihood of a misuse of genetic information, especially by the uninformed who would simply see the information as having potential financial repercussions such as insurers and employers? Would information be kept private or would it be available within schools and the workplace?

Even if we do manage to correlate a person's genetic endowment with behaviour, there will always be other factors involved. As you know, correlations are not an indication of cause and effect. Hasn't this got implications for the future? Supposing we can find a 'murderer gene' – does it automatically mean that a person carrying that gene will develop into a murderer, or might there be some mediating method of preventing the gene from manifesting itself? However, even if there were such a gene, that person would always be regarded with suspicion throughout their lives and this in itself might result in high levels of frustration and some kind of extreme violent act.

Another problem might come if we continue on the path to becoming another 'litigation-state' like the USA, where people can be taken to court for anything and everything, claiming huge sums of money for any slight misdemeanour. Imagine the amount of knowledge that will be required by our solicitors, barristers and judges in order to adjudicate on a case resulting from the incorrect or inappropriate use of genetic information. Forensic DNA evidence is already used in criminal cases or when the identity of the father of a child is brought into question. We will soon be able to discriminate between individuals on the basis of their genetic make-up, and perhaps people will no longer be seen as having free choice.

THE MAJOR ACHIEVEMENTS OF THE HUMAN GENOME PROJECT ●●●●●●●●●●●●●●●●●●●●●●●●●●●●●●●●

The major achievements of the Genome Project have proved so far to be of great benefit, especially in the area of health. It has given us much greater insights into the workings of the human body and even if it hasn't identified genes for certain traits, it has managed to identify the behaviours associated with genetically transmitted disorders, many of which are horrific and lead to immense suffering and ultimately death. Many would agree that although the work is not yet completed, any assistance into dealing with the myriad of human disorders has to be beneficial.

An example of how effective the Human Genome Project has been in identifying illness-related genes can be shown by the work of the Los Alamos National

Laboratory and the Lawrence Livermore National Laboratory, completed in 1995. They produced the highest resolution physical maps for human chromosomes 16 and 19, respectively. The chromosome 19 map has already contributed to the identification of a genetic defect underlying the disease **myotonic dystrophy**, which is an inherited disorder where the muscles contract but have decreasing power to relax and actually become so weak that they waste away. It can also cause mental deficiency, hair loss and cataracts. Onset of this rare disorder commonly occurs during young adulthood. However, it can occur at any age and is extremely variable in its degree of severity. An unusual feature of this illness is that its symptoms usually become more severe with each successive generation. This is because mistakes in the 'copying' of the gene from one generation to the next result in the amplification of the genetic abnormality. Therefore any means of preventing the continuance of the disorder can only be beneficial to families who would otherwise have to deal not only with the knowledge that they had passed it on to the next generation, but also that it would prove more severe with each successive appearance. The chromosome 19 map has also helped to explain an unusual genetic mechanism that is now known to contribute to the onset of at least nine diseases, including Huntington's disease, which is a debilitating progressive disorder which is characterised by abnormal body movements and degeneration of nerve cells in the cerebrum. In addition, genes involved in olfactory receptors, Alzheimer's disease, and one form of migraine headache, have also been discovered on chromosome 19.

Similarly, a number of genes which have been mapped onto chromosome 16 include the genes involved in Batten's disease which is a fatal, inherited disorder of the nervous system that begins in childhood. Early symptoms usually appear when the child is aged between five and ten and develop problems with vision or seizures. Over time, affected children suffer mental impairment, worsening seizures, and a progressive loss of sight and motor skills. Eventually, they become blind, bedridden, and demented and will usually die by the time they are in their late teens or twenties.

Polycystic kidney disease is another inherited disorder, which causes the kidneys to enlarge due to multiple cysts and consequently cease to function, as are Crohn's disease, a chronic inflammatory disease affecting the whole of the alimentary tract from mouth to anus, forms of breast and prostate cancer, and Fanconi's anaemia which is an inherited condition where sufferers develop bone marrow failure and ultimately life-threatening aplastic anaemia whereby their circulatory systems cannot successfully combat infection. Sufferers are also more prone to leukaemia and have a much higher incidence of cancer than the general population.

The data obtained from the Human Genome Project will be available to both medical and scientific researchers and should ultimately help to prevent or find ways of treating some of these horrific genetically transmitted illnesses. However, with regard to psychological investigations, we are still a long way from understanding the basis of normal behaviour and even further from being able to separate the instances of inherited abilities from those influenced predominantly by the environment. Whether it will ever be possible to get at the exact causes of behaviour remains to be seen, but what we must bear in mind is that the apparent simplicity of the original nature–nurture debate has developed into a far more complex issue over the years.

Consequently, when we address the question of why behaviours have occurred, it is important to remember that many of the simplistic debates of former years, which argued that behaviour was *either* caused by the biological make-up of the person *or* was due to the environment within which they grew up, can no longer be considered to give us an answer of sufficient sophistication. Although many of the more dated arguments focused on predispositions and inherited characteristics, they were far less specific than they are today. As the increase in knowledge of 'genes-for-behaviours' continues, we must constantly be aware that genetics is another potential source of explanation. No longer is it acceptable to consider purely physiological explanations for behaviour, such as the fight/flight mechanism; we should now also bear in mind that there are potentially inherited characteristics or predispositions that certain individuals inherit from their parents.

Different methodologies, different designs

4

> **The good and bad points
> and the other things to consider along the way**
>
> • **Appropriateness of the method used**
>
> • **Procedures and experimental controls**

As any student of psychology is aware, there are a number of different ways of conducting research. Some are more appropriate than others and some are more fun. I suppose that all psychologists have their own favourite methodology – for example cognitive psychologists tend to use the experimental method where they can carefully manipulate what participants do in order to identify different discrete cognitive processes. On the other hand, in the past many of the well-known studies in social psychology used observation as their main methodology, as social psychologists are interested in interactions between people according to different situations. It is worth noting that the perspective of the psychologist will often dictate the methodology – even if, on occasion, it might seem inappropriate.

We must also remember that research which to us might look a bit dodgy may have been set up within tight financial or time constraints and the researchers had to do their best with what they had available. Early researchers would have known less about certain issues that influence research than is known today. An example of this is ethical considerations – they became far more significant after it was realised that participants could be harmed by psychological research.

A ROMP THROUGH VARIOUS RESEARCH METHODOLOGIES ●

In order to remind you of the kinds of issues that are important when evaluating psychological methodologies, we will have a brief romp through the techniques used, looking at their strengths and weaknesses, and add some examples to illustrate the various points. The strength of each of these methods is determined by how appropriate it is to the question you have asked, and also how confident you are in the data you have gathered. You must always evaluate research and decide if there might have been a better way of investigating the topic – perhaps using observation rather than a questionnaire, or an experiment rather than a correlation. Ask yourself, when you look at a methodology, how you would conduct similar research and whether your way would be any better. This will give you an idea of the kinds of problems facing researchers.

It is also necessary to look at how *realistic* the research appears to the participants. If you have conducted any sort of research, you will know that participants don't always take your efforts seriously. If the results of the research are to be considered valid in the real world (ecologically valid) then they must have what is known as either **experimental realism** or **mundane realism** (Carlsmith *et al.*, 1976). Experimental realism is where the experimental set up is effective enough to be taken seriously by the participants, despite its artificiality. Mundane realism is where the situation is as close to real life as possible, and this will obviously be higher if the research is conducted in a field setting.

There is also the problem of the 'Hawthorne Effect', identified by research into **organisational psychology** in a systematic series of work studies conducted at the Hawthorne Plant of the Western Electric Group in the USA.

> The experimental studies were intended to identify the ideal working conditions necessary in order to achieve maximum productivity. A group of five employees had their working conditions systematically changed over a period of two-and-a-half years. The factors that were varied were lighting, heating, amount of hours worked, amount of sleep and consumption of food. No matter how the conditions were manipulated, with each successive change, output increased and remained at the new level even when conditions returned to normal.

Despite efforts to determine the *actual* reason for the changes in productivity, no one factor was identified. The Hawthorne Effect suggests that by simply studying something, a change will occur.

Figure 4.1 *At the Hawthorne plant, the very act of studying its workers seemed enough to bring about change*

There are a number of issues within the topic of methodology which are addressed in the next chapter but are mentioned here – these are **demand characteristics, experimenter effects** and **extraneous** or **confounding variables**. Watch out for them as you continue.

EXPERIMENTS

As you already know, experiments are conducted in order to see if an independent variable, manipulated by the researcher, affects the participants in the study.

A basic example of an experiment would be something simple like whether plants grow with or without water. Two plants would be placed side by side in the same room. One would be watered regularly, the other allowed to dry out. The only thing that is different between the conditions of the two plants is the amount of water they are given. Here the amount of water is the independent variable and the rate of growth is the dependent variable.

Experiments such as this are either conducted in a laboratory where everything can be controlled, or in the field where the research is conducted in the subject's normal environment.

Figure 4.2

Similarly, experiments involving people as the subjects can be carried out in laboratories or in the field – the participants' natural environment. The data gathered by experiments can either be measurements of task performance (like memory tests or reaction times) or it could be data gathered by observing and recording categories of behaviour. Bandura's (1961) study of children's behaviour when exposed to different adult models was an experiment, and the data collected was observational.

Strengths

The main strength of experiments is that they are often the most logical method of identifying the effect of a particular variable on participants. They are more tightly controlled than many other methodologies, thus removing the effect of the majority of **extraneous** variables (see Chapter 5) that could interfere with the results. These extraneous variables could be, for example, unexpected differences between participants, but there are also issues like the time of day, temperature and noise levels, which can all be controlled within an experimental situation (see the next chapter for a more comprehensive discussion).

Field experiments have a higher level of ecological validity than experiments carried out in laboratories because the environment is real and therefore less likely to influence the subject.

Weaknesses

The participants' performance or behaviour may be affected as they may try to work out (often incorrectly) the purpose of the study they are involved in and hence influence the results (demand characteristics – see Chapter 5).

The environment in which an experiment takes place may well affect the participants – laboratories are unfamiliar to most research participants. This in itself may confound the results, which may be due to the participants' response to a strange environment and not the independent variable being manipulated.

Field experiments, though more realistic, have the problem of not being so easily controlled.

The researcher may influence the subjects either in the way he/she behaves or in the way he/she records the data (experimenter effects – see Chapter 5). Another problem with any kind of experiment is that the task participants are asked to do may well be unfamiliar to them, for example a 'reaction time' test, or one in which subjects are required to visually manipulate three-dimensional objects.

Another problem is that there may be differences between the groups of participants involved in the study. Participants in one set of experimental conditions may all be very intelligent, or perhaps all male or all very young and so on.

Research designs

In order to counteract the last problem, there are a number of different research designs which can be used. These are detailed below.

Repeated measures: One way to carry out research that would remove the effect of subject variables would be to use a **repeated measures design**. Here, participants take part in all experimental conditions and so the subject variables are perfectly balanced. However, if the difference between the conditions can only be experienced over time, the time delay may also have an effect on the participants. One example is comparing living in an area with low levels of pollution with living in another area with high levels of pollution. Age, maturity and experience can also influence the results, especially if the participants are children.

The other problem with this design is that the results might become contaminated by **order effects.** These are where the order in which tasks are undertaken may have an effect on the results. Probably the best way to describe an order effect is to imagine that participants in a study are asked to undertake two memory tests. They have to memorise two lists of words, one after the other. However, the words they remember from the first list may influence the words they remember from the second list. For example, below are two potential lists for memorising. You may think my example is quite strange, but it will demonstrate how order effects work. Participants are expected to learn and then recall both lists, probably doing something different in between like drinking caffeinated coffee or running round the block. Let us assume that they do it in the following order:

List 1	List 2
Book	Work
Tree	Friday
Heron	Apple
Bottle	Dinner
Table	Potato
Car	Shoe
Window	Fly
Park	Pencil
Fork	Plug
Stone	Curtain
Camera	Glasses
Officer	Flowers
Home	Iron
Company	Card
Egg	Feather

The word 'car' appears in the first list. If I were doing this particular memory test, it is likely that I would remember the word 'plug' from the second list, because I would make an association between cars and plugs – cars have spark plugs. (This is because the spark plugs in my car have just been changed – it's running much more smoothly now rather than misfiring and sounding like it's about to die at any minute.) Another person might associate the word 'plug' with the plug you put in a sink, so they would not have had the cue from the first list to help them remember it. Supposing someone else kept chickens; they might have had a cue from the word 'egg' to the word 'feather'. If at least half the participants do one list first then the other, and the rest do them the other way round, then these order effects would hopefully be ironed out. This method of dealing with order effects is called **counterbalancing**, whereby some participants do the tasks in one order and the remaining participants do them in the opposite order.

Supposing the tasks to be undertaken both involve using a certain skill. In this case participants' scores may become affected by **practice effects** – the effects of doing something once and then being better at it the next time due to having had some practice. However, if participants carry out two or more activities in rapid succession they may well become tired – known as **fatigue effects.** You can imagine how this might interfere with research into an area such as **sports psychology,** for example the effect of teaching method on the learning of a particular skill. Any increased level of skill by the athlete is as likely to be due to practice as to a change in the teaching method used!

Figure 4.3 Practice makes perfect

Independent subjects: Another way of minimising variation between groups of participants is to use an **independent subjects design**. This is where a group of participants are allocated randomly to two groups. The weakness of this design is immediately obvious because there may be considerable variation between the subjects in each group.

Therefore it is best used when there are large numbers of available participants. The idea is that if you randomly divide a large sample into two groups, the differences between the groups balance themselves out. You would therefore expect to get a relatively representative sample of your population in each group and could therefore confidently assume that any differences between the groups were due to the experimental conditions rather than to the characteristics of the people involved. But I wonder how many independent subject designs really do have sufficient numbers in their samples to iron out any differences between them?

The following examples are of two experiments from the area of **environmental psychology** and illustrate some of the evaluative issues, both positive and negative, that might be relevant to such research:

Research into the effects of noise on helping behaviour was undertaken by Mathews and Canon in 1975 and to do this they set up a laboratory experiment and then a field experiment.

Experiment 1

Individual subjects were exposed to one of a number of different levels of noise through a hidden speaker while they waited in a laboratory to take part in an experiment. They had no idea what the experiment was about. They were not alone because a confederate of the researcher was waiting with them, seated with a pile of papers on their lap, supposedly reading a journal. The subjects believed this confederate was also a potential subject. The researcher entered the laboratory and called the confederate who stood up, dropping the papers right in front of the subject. The dependent variable was whether or not the subject helped the confederate and it was found that, the louder the noise, the less likely the subject was to help.

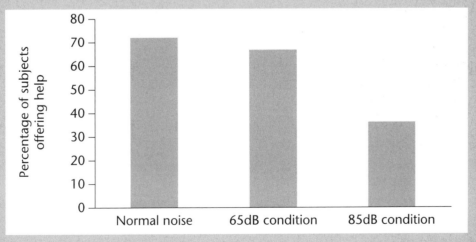

Figure 4.4 *Fewer people helped in the noisy condition*

Experiment 2

The second part of the experiment involved a slightly more complicated design. The confederate of the researcher would drop a box of books as he got out of a car. The independent variable of noise was manipulated by having a lawn mower with its engine running near the event, giving a volume of 87 dB compared with 50 dB when it was 'parked'. The 50 dB was the normal street noise level. In half the trials, the confederate had a plaster cast on his arm. The idea was to see whether need influenced helping or whether noise was the overriding issue here.

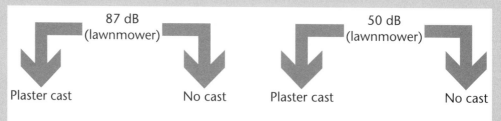

Figure 4.5

The results showed that noise had little effect on helping behaviour when the subject didn't have a cast on. In fact there was little difference between the lawnmower and no lawnmower condition – people helped 10 per cent of the time with the lawnmower running and 20 per cent when it wasn't running. However, when the confederate wore the plaster cast, people helped 80 per cent of the time in the 'no lawnmower' condition, but only 15 per cent in the 'lawnmower' condition.

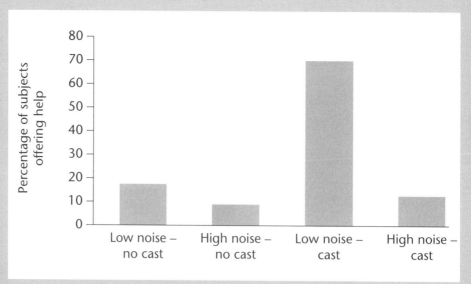

Figure 4.6 Here noise is more important than the needs of the person

In both of these experiments, although the independent variable was manipulated effectively by the researchers, there are a number of issues which are quite obvious.

- Did the participant in Experiment 1 feel comfortable in the laboratory setting or was it an unfamiliar environment? Although we cannot be sure, it is possible that the participant would have some knowledge of the environment, bearing in mind that the majority of participants in research in the USA in the 1970s were white, middle class, undergraduate students. On the other hand, he/she may have felt anxious as they were waiting to undergo the test, and would probably have been a little nervous as a result.

- In Experiment 1 the volume of noise could be manipulated effectively, and the behaviour of researcher and confederate would have been almost identical in all trials. In contrast, Experiment 2 was more ecologically valid because the participant was in a familiar environment and was not brought into a laboratory to 'perform'. However, the volume of the noise could not be controlled so effectively – there may also have been other noises that were not taken into account.

- The 'condition' of the participants in Experiment 2 would have varied as with most opportunity samples. Some would have been in a hurry, and others perhaps willing to help because they had nothing better to do. There may have been other factors affecting the results such as the hearing acuity of the participants, the location of the lawnmower in relation to the person dropping the book, and the fact that each trial might have varied slightly in the way it was carried out and the conditons prevailing at the time. People not involved in the study could also have been given the chance to intervene, and this might have influenced the results.

Matched pairs: The final way of reducing differences between the groups of participants is to match them – that is, to make them as similar as possible by matching them on the factors that are considered important. These factors could be age, gender, ability, personality or whatever. Studies which look at different groups of people operating in different conditions have to make sure that their participants are matched. An example of some research, taken from **environmental psychology**, showing why it is necessary to match participants, is given below.

Cohen *et al.* (1973) were interested in the effects of noise on the performance of children. In order to measure performance, they decided to look at reading ability. They studied children living in a large high-rise apartment complex situated over a noisy highway in New York City, and discovered (not surprisingly) that the noise on the lower floors was more severe than on the upper floors.

They found that the children from the lower floors had a poorer reading performance and hearing discrimination than the children on the upper floors.

Although this study did not involve the manipulation of the independent variable – the noise pollution (i.e. it was a quasi-experiment), it illustrates how other factors may affect the results. The participants will have been subjected to different amounts of air pollution, and may even have come from different social backgrounds. After all, the closer you are to traffic the more likely you are to be exposed to high levels of carbon monoxide, and presumably the noisier, more polluted flats were occupied by people on lower incomes. Both of these would have been confounding factors. However, the researchers controlled for social class and air pollution, which made the findings far more valid. There are other factors which may also have influenced the results, such as family position (oldest vs youngest child), innate intelligence, confidence to perform in reading tests and so on, but at least some of the confounding variables (see Chapter 5) had been controlled.

Another example from environmental psychology, which may have been influenced by differences in the groups of participants, was an investigation of the effects of personal space on the disclosure of information.

Stone and Morden (1976) investigated how the distance you sit from a therapist influences the amount of information you are willing to disclose. The participants sat at either two feet, five feet or nine feet from the therapist and it was found that they volunteered the most personal information at the five-foot distance and that if that distance was varied, it produced negative effects.

Figure 4.7 Is this a comfortable distance? Imagine sitting in the armchair in the background

It is possible that the participants who were asked to sit in close proximity to the therapist had a greater requirement for personal space because they were of a certain personality type (**introverts** require more space than **extroverts** according to Cook, (1970) and Patterson and Holmes (1966)). There may also have been differences in their personal experiences, with some having more personal information to volunteer than others.

In order to evaluate research in terms of the methodology used, apply the following questions to the study:

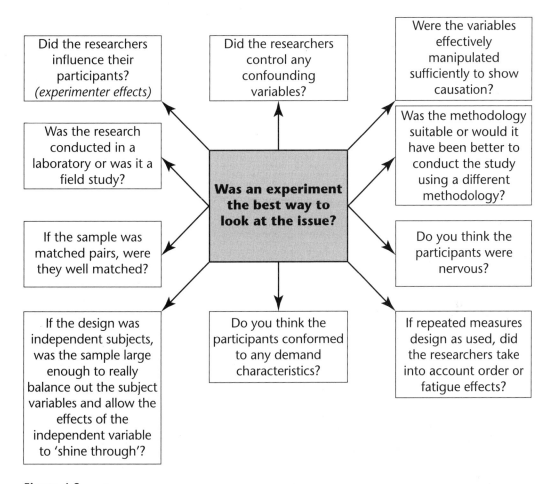

Figure 4.8

OBSERVATIONS ●

When talking about observational methods of research, it is necessary to differentiate between using **observation** as a technique within another design (for example, watching where someone chooses to sit down in an experiment in which you have manipulated the seating) and using observation as an overall research method in which you watch and categorise the naturally occurring behaviour of people in a specific setting. The associated problems with observation, such as accuracy, can be controlled by having a well-designed observation schedule in which the behaviours under observation are well defined. The level of accuracy can be increased by having more than one observer. The level of agreement between observers is known as **inter-observer reliability**. The accepted level of inter-observer or inter-rater reliability is about 95 per cent.

Ideally, observations give us a much more realistic picture of the behaviour of a person, free from the constraints that might be introduced with some types of experimental method. They can be undertaken in a laboratory or in a natural environment, and can involve the use of overt, covert or participant observation.

- **Overt observations** are where the participants know they are being observed, for example Green (1985) found that black pupils in schools received less time and attention from teachers than white pupils.
- **Covert observations** are where the participants are unaware of the observers or the fact that they may be being filmed by hidden cameras, for example Piliavin's (1969) subway study involved the researchers secretly observing from further down the train carriage.
- **Participant observations** are where the researcher interacts with the people he/she is observing although they may or may not be aware of the reason for his/her presence, for example Rosenhan's (1973) study which aimed to discover whether psychiatric hospitals could tell the sane from the insane. He recruited eight people who agreed to try and gain admittance to psychiatric hospitals and then observe the responses they received from the medical staff once 'inside'.

Strengths

The strengths of the observational method lie in the fact that observing behaviour (especially in a naturalistic environment) can often give us more valid information about a person than putting someone in a manipulated environment and asking them to do specific tasks where they know they are the focus of some kind of investigation. Ethologists claim that behaviour that is not observed in a naturalistic setting is very easily misinterpreted as it is seen as separate from the normal chain of events. I always think of the example of a fox and dog digging. The observed behaviour is the same but the reason for the digging is likely to be very different. One is digging a home and the other is burying a bone.

Weaknesses

Unless the categories of observation are carefully defined, it is likely that behaviour might be misinterpreted. The study below, taken from the area of **criminal psychology**, might be open to all sorts of problems.

Feshback and Singer (1971) investigated the effects of showing different types of films to over 600 boys living in boys' homes, to see whether some films resulted in an increase in violent behaviour. The boys came from three private residential schools for middle class boys and four residential treatment homes for boys lacking proper home care. The boys were shown what the researchers categorised as either six hours of violent television (the 'violent' group) or six hours of non-violent television (the 'neutral' group) over a period of six weeks (plus additional hours of assigned programmes if required). During the six weeks they observed the behaviour of the boys to look for differing levels of aggression. They found that the aggression of the 'violent' group was almost half that of the 'neutral' group. The reason for this, they concluded, was that the violent television was having a cathartic effect on the boys.

Figure 4.9 *Does TV really affect our behaviour?*

If you are considering the effectiveness of a study you need to ask yourself a number of questions and we will use the Feshback and Singer study to illustrate what questions we could ask.

1 How did the researchers categorise violent behaviour and can we be sure that there was no violent behaviour in what were called the 'non-violent' programmes?
2 How often did they observe the boys because this may have influenced their decisions? (In fact, a member of staff completed a behaviour rating scale daily).

3 Did the boys know they were being watched? If the boys who watched the violent television programmes were aware that it was not socially acceptable to demonstrate aggressive behaviour, even though the television raised their arousal levels, they may well conduct their violent demonstrations out of the sight of the researchers.

There were other concerns about the study, which incidentally has not been replicated. There was no assessment of the levels of violence in the non-violent programmes and it turned out that violent cartoons were actually shown in the non-violent condition. Also, there was no measure of how attentive the children were to the programmes. Finally, some teenage boys expressed annoyance and frustration that they couldn't watch their favourite programmes, which in itself may have lead to frustration and ultimately higher demonstrations of aggressive behaviour.

Another weakness of observational research relates to the misperception of a behaviour. For example, **expectancy bias** is where the researcher is expecting to see a certain behaviour and is therefore biased towards it.

Research into **criminal psychology** indicates that we are very much influenced by stereotypes. One example of this is the suggestion that the race of a defendant may have some influence on how likely they are to be perceived as guilty.

> Research by Pfeifer and Ogloff (1991) indicated that university students were more likely to believe black defendants were guilty of a crime compared with white defendants.

In this case, expectancy bias would influence the students' interpretation of any observed behaviour they may witness in the future.

Another weakness with any sort of overt observation is the potential for **experimenter effects**, caused simply by the reaction of the participants to the presence of the researcher. For example, participants who know they are being observed may not act normally, or the researcher may actually influence their behaviour more directly (if, say, they are participant observers). If the participants have some idea about the intentions of the research, they might act according to **demand characteristics**. I often wonder if people who are encouraged to take part in health promotion programmes as part of a research study do so only because they know their behaviour is being closely monitored and they feel under pressure to take part.

In order to evaluate research in terms of the methodology used, apply the questions in Figure 4.10 to the study.

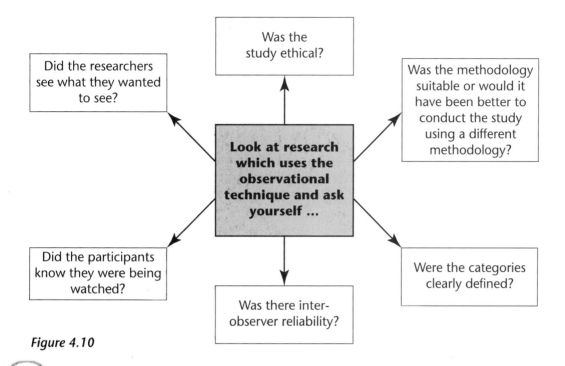

Figure 4.10

CASE STUDIES •

Case studies are the in-depth study of an individual or very small group of people, usually over a prolonged period of time. The studies themselves may be retrospective or current, following the behaviours of an individual or small group over the course of time. A common type of case study in applied psychology looks at the long-term behaviour of a person with an unusual or rare type of disorder. Here the case study can be used to gain insight into the nature and aetiology of the condition and therefore help to alleviate the effects of the condition on the person involved.

There are a number of examples of case studies which are familiar to students of psychology, such as Freud's (1909) study of the phobia of Little Hans or Thigpen and Cleckley's (1954) study of the multiple personalities of Eve White. There are many more case studies such as that of Peter Sutcliffe, also known as the Yorkshire Ripper, who murdered 13 women in the north of England between 1975 and 1981. Burns (1985), in his book *Somebody's Husband, Somebody's Son*, looked at Sutcliffe's social background and life experiences and helped to piece together explanations for his subsequent behaviour.

Strengths

The strengths of case studies lie in the fact that they allow us to look at a person's behaviour over a long period of time, in different situations and in depth. This makes it likely that the causes and mediating influences on that behaviour can be identified, and further researched using some kind of experiment.

Figure 4.11 Case studies of notorious criminals like Peter Sutcliffe make persuasive reading, but how objective are they likely to be?
© News of the World

Weaknesses

The main weaknesses of a case study are that the researcher may be subjective in his/her interpretation of the person's behaviour.

In order to evaluate research in terms of the methodology used, apply the questions in Figure 4.12 to the study.

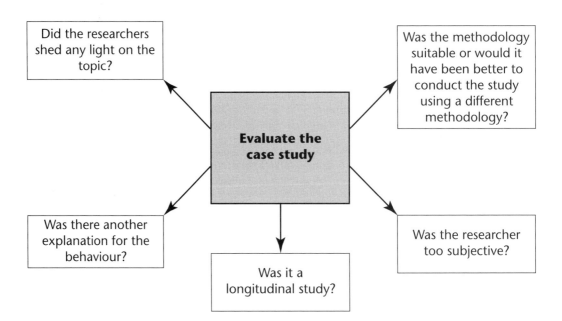

Did the researchers shed any light on the topic?

Was the methodology suitable or would it have been better to conduct the study using a different methodology?

Evaluate the case study

Was there another explanation for the behaviour?

Was it a longitudinal study?

Was the researcher too subjective?

Figure 4.12

SURVEYS, QUESTIONNAIRES, INTERVIEWS • • • • • • • • •

Surveys, questionnaires and interviews are used either to support other evidence gathered by researchers or to find out about emotions, attitudes and lifestyles. Surveys are generally broad data-gathering exercises which ask large numbers of people what their attitudes, opinions and feelings are about certain issues. Questionnaires and interviews may be used to find out more specific information; however, they *must* use questions which are understood by the participants or the data collected will be of no use at all.

The format of these methods can be **open** or **closed questions**, **rating scales** or **multiple choice questions**. As you and I both know, the fixed choice questions can be really irritating because you often want to write NONE OF THESE and then fill in your own answer, but this provides the researcher with a huge problem; how to analyse unstructured data.

Questionnaires generally have closed questions whereas interviews are often used to get at more in-depth information. Whatever the format, they should be easy to understand, interpret and even have some sort of lie scale built in (because people are often unwilling to disclose information which might result in them being judged unfavourably, they may give socially desirable answers as opposed to the true ones).

Such methods are used regularly in areas such as **health psychology**, where it is important to try and identify attitudes and behaviour in terms of treating illnesses. One area, identifying stress levels, uses a number of different rating scales such as the **Social Readjustment Rating Scale** (see Table 4.1) (Holmes and Rahe, 1967) and the **Hassles Scale** (Kanner *et al.*, 1981). These are questionnaires that give lists of events which act as 'stressors', and ask participants to identify events which have occurred in their lives. These are either given a rating score (Social Readjustment Rating Scale) or are rated by the participant for severity of result.

As Banyard (1996) points out, there are a number of problems with the SRRS. You are told to tick off the events which have happened to you during a specified time, such as twelve months or two years, and, according to Holmes and Rahe, the higher the score the more chance you have of developing an illness. However, major life events are quite rare and so many of us will have very low scores although we may still feel stressed and develop illnesses. There are also problems interpreting what is meant by some of the events, and not all of them apply to every person, for example an unmarried 20-year-old is unlikely to experience a son or daughter leaving home!

I suppose one of the biggest questions here is whether it is possible to simply conduct a pencil and paper test to gather information about, say, people's emotions, and then use this to predict subsequent behaviour or responses. Although there is evidence that questionnaires can be effective in identifying a number of factors, we

Table 4.1 *The Social Readjustment Rating Scale*

Life event	Mean value
Death of a spouse	100
Divorce	73
Marital separation	65
Jail term	63
Death of close family member	63
Personal injury or illness	53
Marriage	50
Fired at work	47
Marital reconciliation	45
Retirement	45
Change in health of family member	44
Pregnancy	40
Sex difficulties	39
Gain of new family member	39
Business readjustment	39
Change in financial state	38
Death of close friend	37
Change to different line of work	36
Change in number of arguments with spouse	35
Mortgage over $10,000	31
Foreclosure of mortgage or loan	30
Change in responsibilities at work	29
Son or daughter leaving home	29
Trouble with in-laws	29
Outstanding personal achievement	28
Wife begins or stops work	26
begin or end school	26
Change in living conditions	25
Revisions of personal habits	24
Trouble with boss	23
Change in work hours or conditions	20
Change in residence	20
Change in schools	20
Change in recreation	19
Change in church activities	19
Change in social activities	18
Mortgage or loan less than $10,000	17
Change in sleeping habits	16
Change in number of family get-togethers	15
Change in eating habits	15
Vacation	13
Christmas	12
Minor violations of the law	11

must remember that the answers given may not be the true ones. For example, people can often judge which answers will make them appear in the most favourable light. How can you really find out how someone feels or what state they are in by asking them blunt and controlled questions? This may be the value of interviews over pencil and paper exercises, but in this case the subjectivity of the interviewer may mask the scientific validity of the investigation.

Strengths

Surveys and questionnaires are useful for gathering large quantities of data. They are easy to administer and, if designed carefully, easy to analyse and check for 'lies'. Interviews, especially if they contain open-ended questions, allow researchers to explore areas which might give a deeper insight into behaviour.

Weaknesses

Generally the greatest weakness with any of these methods is that people may not give honest answers. They may give socially acceptable responses, or even try to shock the researcher by conforming to stereotypes. Rating scales are probably the most accurate pencil and paper test of peoples' attitudes because they allow a number of choices. However, if the rating scale is a five-point Likert scale (see below), for example, there is a likelihood that the participants who do not take the research seriously will pick the third choice.

1	2	3	4	5
Good				Bad

One way around this is to have a six-point scale (or any even scale) in order to force answers in one direction or another:

1	2	3	4	5	6
Good					Bad

However, you always get the really annoying person who draws an extra line down the middle on purpose!

Surveys and questionnaires

People are often unwilling to take part in surveys unless there is some kind of reward. Therefore it is likely that the sample will be a 'self-selecting survey-friendly' sample and probably not representative of the population as a whole.

Interviews

The person who is conducting the interview may influence the responses of the participants. For example, a group of young men convicted of an offence may well respond differently to a middle-aged, middle-class woman than to a younger, tougher, working-class man who had obviously been around and wouldn't be easily shocked. This must be considered when looking at the responses of participants to interviews. The next example, again taken from the field of **criminal psychology**, might give you an idea of what I mean.

> Browne and Pennell (1997) interviewed young offenders before and after they had watched a violent film. They concluded that the violence shown is interpreted differently by the offenders depending on their backgrounds; offenders from violent backgrounds who show low levels of empathy read the violence in a different way to offenders that come from non-violent backgrounds.

I wonder if the researchers affected the offenders in any way? Perhaps the offenders wanted to shock the researchers, or were they conforming to their idea of the stereotypical offender? Also, how did the researchers determine the offenders levels of empathy – did they ask them, or did they observe them?

In order to evaluate research in terms of the methodology used, apply the following questions to the study:

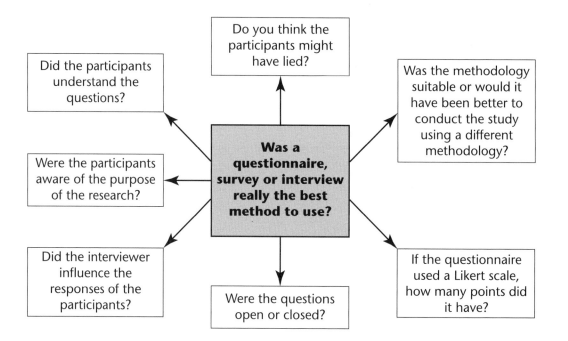

Figure 4.13

PHYSIOLOGICAL MEASUREMENTS ● ● ● ● ● ● ● ● ● ● ● ● ● ● ●

The measurement of physiological response is perhaps the most scientific technique, in so far as it is objective and conducted using equipment which is not open to mis-interpretation or misrepresentation; it also lacks any form of subjectivity. This method involves actually assessing the activity of the nervous system by either look-ing at brain structure and function whilst the subject is undertaking a task, or analysing the presence or absence of neurotransmitters (chemical messengers). All physiological techniques require the use of carefully designed instruments and accu-rate equipment.

- **EEGs (electroencephalograms)** measure the changes in electrical activity in dif-ferent areas of the brain by recording from electrodes placed on the surface of the brain.
- **CT (computerised tomography)** is a refined version of an X-ray in which the patient is moved slowly through a doughnut-shaped CT machine while the X-ray tube rotates around the body, sending beams from all directions. This produces a number of successive cross-sectional images of the area under investigation which are clearer than ordinary X-rays.
- **MRI scans** produce high-contrast images of soft tissue in areas where X-rays and CT scans are weak. They can distinguish body tissues from each other on the basis of differences in their water content that the tissues contain. For example the brain is made up of fatty white matter and more watery grey matter, and these can be easily distinguished using MRI scans. They are ideal for detecting tumours and degenerative diseases.
- **PET scans** allow researchers to examine the relationship between brain activity and mental processes by analysing gamma-ray emissions from areas of the brain which are most active. The patient has an injection of radioisotopes that have been tagged to biological molecules such as glucose. The more active brain cells use more glucose than surrounding areas, and this is detected and fed into a computer, producing a live-action picture of the brain's biochemical activity.
- Researchers can also measure **galvanic skin response**, which is a measure of the skin's conductivity. When we become aroused or anxious, we perspire more than normal and this change is sufficient to increase the electrical conductivity of the skin. If two electrodes are placed on the skin, this level of conductivity can be measured to give an indication of the activity of the autonomic nervous system.
- Measures of **blood pressure** and **heart rate** can also give an indication of levels of autonomic arousal.
- **Biochemical analysis** of blood samples may indicate high or low levels of cer-tain substances such as blood sugars or adrenaline.

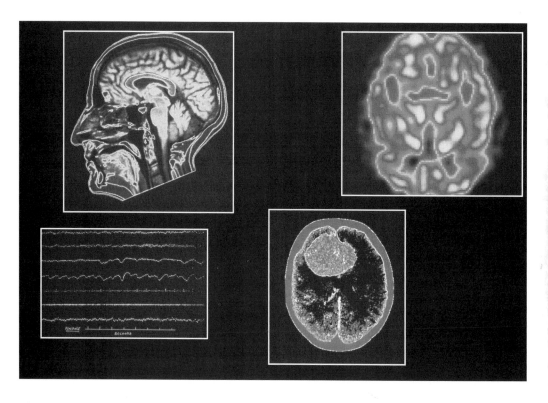

Figure 4.14 *From top left clockwise, an MRI scan, a PET scan, a CT scan and EEG*

One example of a study which used physiological measurements as a way of looking at brain activity is from the area of **criminal psychology**. Raine *et al.* (1997) looked at the activity of murderers' brains.

The study involved looking to see if there was any difference in brain functioning, using PET scans, between a group of murderers who pleaded not guilt by reason of insanity and a carefully matched control group. The expectation was that the 'murderers' would show evidence of brain dysfunction in their prefrontal cortex, as well as in other areas that have been linked to violent behaviour in the past. All the participants were kept medication-free for two weeks prior to the brain scanning.

The 'murderers' were injected with a radioactive tracer and their brain activity was compared with that of a control group whilst undertaking a task which involved the activity of the frontal lobes. Although there was no significant overall difference in task performance between the two groups, there was evidence of a significant difference in glucose metabolism in a number of areas of the brain, especially in the frontal lobes which control higher order functioning.

This study indicates that there could be a physiological cause of murderous behaviour. What we now need to ask is whether the behaviour we have identified was caused by damage to the brain, or was the brain damage caused by the behaviour? Let me explain what I mean by this. I am going to use the example of Genie, the young girl studied by Curtis (1977) who was raised in isolation up to the age of thirteen, when she was discovered. She was unable to talk (having been beaten for making any noise) and looked and behaved like a very young child. Her father claimed that she had been born brain damaged and he hid her away believing that she would die by the age of twelve. However, whether or not she was brain damaged at birth could never be proved as the lack of stimulation and opportunity to vocalise for thirteen years may well have resulted in her brain failing to develop. It was apparent that she had brain damage, but was she born with it, or was it caused by her thirteen years of the isolation and abuse? We will never know.

Therefore, when looking at the functioning of the brain, we cannot automatically conclude that brain function alone is the cause of behaviour. The idea of biological determinism – that our behaviour is determined by our biology – must be considered alongside past experiences and societal pressures.

Strengths

All methods used to measure our biological responses involve the use of specialised scientific equipment, so differences in response can be measured objectively rather than relying on the interpretation of the researcher.

Weaknesses

The problem with using any kind of equipment is that some people find it quite unnerving. Consider the most simple equipment – a blood pressure machine (sphygmomanometer), which consists of a cuff around the arm to measure blood pressure. When the cuff begins to inflate it is sometimes uncomfortable, and the person may begin to feel nervous. This nervousness, in physiological terms, is related to arousal. If we are aroused, our autonomic nervous system activity increases and our blood pressure, heart rate and so on also increase. Is the measurement therefore really a reflection of our response to the experimental conditions, or is it simply related to the equipment being used to measure it? Now apply this idea to an experiment involving a machine that takes PET scans, or having an injection of radioisotopes …

More research has indicated that there could be a number of physiological causes of behaviours, besides that measured by the functioning of the cortex, but many of these present methodological problems due to the large numbers of confounding variables involved.

In order to evaluate research in terms of the methodology used, apply the following questions to the study:

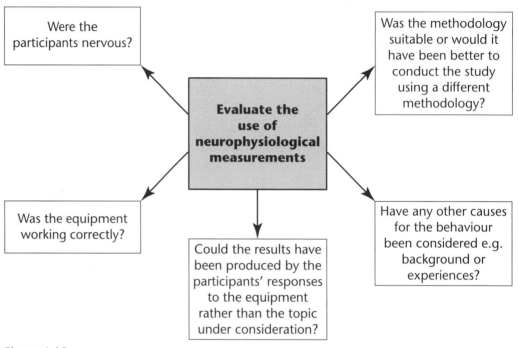

Figure 4.15

CORRELATIONS

Although correlation is not so much a design but more of a statistical procedure, it is often used in psychological research when looking at the relationship between two variables. A common correlation is the amount of violent television watched and the aggressive behaviour of the viewer. As I am sure you are aware, there are a great number of factors that might contribute to the level of violence displayed by the viewer – things like family experiences, and a tendency to violent behaviour. Although a correlation can indicate a relationship between two variables, it does not show cause and effect.

Another example would be whether there is a relationship between the physical strength of an athlete and his or her speed of running. Our initial reaction would be to say 'yes, that makes sense', but on the other hand that would imply that all athletes should be very strong. You only have to look at some of the long-distance runners who actually look quite thin and scrawny to realise that although there may well be a correlation between the two, the relationship is not necessarily causal.

Strengths

Correlations can be used to indicate if there is a relationship between two variables, and form the basis for further research.

Weaknesses

Correlations do not show cause and effect.

> An example of correlational evidence comes from a study in the area of **educational and environmental psychology** which looked at whether the distance between a teacher and student is likely to affect learning.
>
> Research by Sommer (1969), looking at effects of seating position in a circle, found that students who were seated directly opposite the teacher participated the most in seminar-type discussions. The ones who sat at the sides participated the next most frequently, whilst the ones who sat next to the instructor (shoulder to shoulder) tended not to participate at all.

The conclusion here is that seating position influences interaction, but why? It may have been that the personalities of the students influenced where they sat, and that their personalities were therefore responsible for their participation rather than seating position. Eye contact may also have influenced participation far more than seating choice – it is easier to look at the people sitting opposite you than adjacent to you, therefore you are more likely to interact with them. It is obvious that there is some kind of relationship here, but what *causes* it needs to be teased out of the findings, and this can only be done with further research.

Another example is a study which comes from the area of **organisational psychology**, which looked at the relationship between the physical appearance of a person and how likely they are to succeed.

> Buchanan and Huczynski (1997) in their book *Organisational Behaviour* talked about the physical attribute of height and cited a recent British study which showed a relationship between stature and earnings. They suggested that for each four inches of height in adolescence, earnings rose by two per cent in early adulthood.

However, I can think of a few other factors besides height which might be related to earnings, for example, personality type, attractiveness, intelligence, self-esteem and skill. After all, many of today's famous actors are actually very short – think of Michael J. Fox and Tom Cruise.

Figure 4.16 Tom Cruise

In order to evaluate research in terms of the methodology used, apply the following questions to the study:

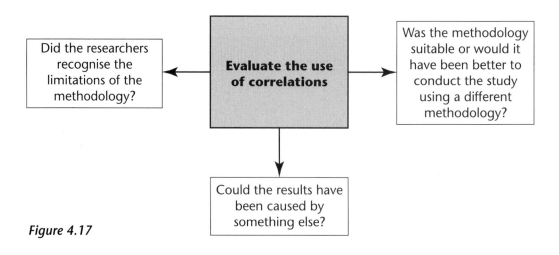

| Did the researchers recognise the limitations of the methodology? | ← | **Evaluate the use of correlations** | → | Was the methodology suitable or would it have been better to conduct the study using a different methodology? |

Could the results have been caused by something else?

Figure 4.17

SAMPLES •

We have now looked at different methodologies and considered some of their strengths and weaknesses. Another important factor is the sample chosen for the research. After all, there would be no point in choosing a sample that was not relevant to the research. Generally speaking, studying little old ladies doesn't actually help us a great deal if we are looking at the personality of people who have recently been found guilty of some kind of crime!

In fact, identifying a population of people you are interested in presents few problems. Similarly, deciding upon a method of selecting those people for study is also an easy decision to make – in theory. The problem arises when you actually try to put these decisions into practice. People who would make ideal participants for the research may refuse to take part, perhaps because they think the research is pointless, or because they feel nervous and don't want to be judged, or simply because they have better things to do. Different research uses different samples and these can have a profound effect on the results of the research.

The ideal sample is generally thought to be a **random sample**, where every member of the population you have identified has an equal chance of being chosen. The problem is that random samples may have random errors – though **quota samples** can reduce this random error effect. By this I mean that a random sample may end up being unrepresentative since, by chance, it contains, for example, mainly younger participants, whereas quota sampling would actually identify the different sub-groups required and then specify equal numbers of people to be selected from each sub-group. To improve the sample still further, a **stratified sample** would give the right proportions of people from each sub-group (or strata) in order to represent the population as a whole.

The last technique I will mention here is known as **snowball sampling**, although it is more commonly used when researchers simply want to get an overview of a particular situation such as the use of drugs in a certain area, or bullying in a school, or even the way an organisation functions. This involves the researcher selecting a number of people they believe are of particular relevance to the issue under investigation, and then following up any other potential contacts who may have been suggested as a result of the original interviews. You can immediately see that this technique could be highly subjective, in contrast to the more objective techniques we are used to dealing with in psychological research. However, as research is moving more to favouring qualitative as well as quantitative studies, this technique may become more common in the future.

As I said earlier, you may select your participants, but whether they agree to take part or not is a different matter. Self-selecting samples (samples of people who actively choose to take part in the research) are unlikely to be representative of the population you are interested in. (There will be something about them that makes them more likely to volunteer.) The other method used by researchers is what is known as an opportunity sample – one which is extremely familiar to psychology students. These are people who hapen to be present at the time the sample is chosen and are willing to take part.

In fact, many of the participants who have taken part in psychological research in the past (especially social psychological research) have been white, middle-class, male undergraduate psychology students. Often, the reason they volunteer for studies is as a way of gaining credits for their courses or of opting out of doing essays – hardly representative of the population as a whole! In fact, Sears (1986) pointed out that between the 1960s and 1980s, most psychological research was undertaken using laboratory studies with students as subjects. To highlight the extent of this use of 'non-representative' samples, a review article of research which had been published in American journals in 1980 pointed out that 46 per cent of studies involved psychology students as participants, 37 per cent involved other students and only 17 per cent of studies used adults. We could argue here that not only are they not representative of people in general, they are also not representative of the people of America either!

I wonder how many of the American student participants were coerced into taking part in the various research projects, and if so, how accurate was the data they provided? It is also relevant to take into account the ethics of pressurising students to participate (if this is what happened) to the extent that they did not have a free choice.

Would the sample be representative if researchers were to offer some kind of financial reward for participating? This indicates that the kind of people who would volunteer may come from a group that is less well off, and therefore only represent one section of society. In fact it has been found that volunteer rates do increase the greater the incentives offered. If, on the other hand, researchers advertised for participants, the participants would be selected from a sampling frame of people who read advertisements in that particular publication.

Using volunteers who are offered no incentives for participating in the research overcomes many of the ethical problems that arise if payment is offered in the form of money or credits on university courses. People involved on voluntary basis would not feel so awkward if they decided half-way through the research to withdraw than if they'd been paid to take part. The obvious problem with this kind of participant is that they too may fail to represent the population under investigation. In fact, Rosenthal and Rosnow (1991) found that it was possible to distinguish volunteers from other research participants. They discovered that volunteers seem to have a number of distinguishing characteristics that presumably make them more likely to agree to take part in psychological research. It is these characteristics which, as you will see, make them less representative of the population as a whole.

Table 4.2 *A table showing how confident Rosenthal and Rosnow were when suggesting the likely characteristics of volunteers: adapted from* Essentials of Behavioural Research: Methods and Data Analysis *(1991, 2nd edition)*

Maximum confidence	**Considerable confidence**	**Some confidence**
Educated	Arousal-seeking	From smaller town
Higher social class	Unconventional	Interested in religion
Intelligent	Female	Altruistic
Approval-motivated	Non-authoritarian	Self-disclosing
Sociable	Jewish/Protestant/Catholic	Maladjusted
	Non-conforming	Young

Rosenthal and Rosnow discovered considerable evidence to suggest that volunteers possess all of the first group of characteristics (educated, higher social class and so on), and slightly less from the second group. There is some evidence that volunteers can be described by the third group, although it is not as strong as for the other two groups.

Let's look at the characteristics of volunteers and how they might influence research findings. We are intending to find a standardised score of intelligence for a section of the population (remember – a standardised score is a kind of group norm or mean score which we can use to compare against other scores to give us an idea of how 'normal' someone is). We advertise for volunteers in the 35–50 age group with the intention of gaining a relatively large number of people from which to calculate our standardised score. The people who volunteer, according to Rosenthal and Rosnow, are likely to be educated and more intelligent than the population as a whole. Therefore the standardised score we calculate is unlikely to be truly representative of the population of 35- to 50-year-olds.

Now consider the characteristic of 'approval-motivation' for a moment. If we were conducting research and our participants were high in approval-motivation, it would mean that they would behave in order to gain approval, and not necessarily how they would want to behave – they would be likely to conform to **demand characteristics**. This could have a serious effect on the results of the research, for example with health promotion campaigns. Participants would be tempted to rate the campaigns as excellent (even when they weren't) in order to gain the approval of the researchers. They would also be likely to learn quickly from the campaign (because they are more intelligent than the population as a whole) and this would make the campaigns seem more effective than they would be normally.

The following study from the area of **health psychology** is an example of how presenting information and inducing different levels of fear can influence participants' later behaviours.

Janis and Feshbach (1953) investigated the effectiveness of persuasive communications containing different levels of fear-inducing information. The student participants were randomly assigned to one of four groups (three experimental groups and one control group). The experimental groups were presented with three different 15-minute lectures on the dangers of tooth decay, whereby the independent variable of 'fear level' was manipulated by the information given in the lectures. The strong fear condition heard 71 references to unpleasant effects, the moderate heard 49 and the low fear condition heard just 18.

Immediately after the presentation of information the students rated the high fear message as the most interesting but after a week, the low fear message seemed to be the one that had caused the most change in their attitudes and health-related behaviour.

Although this study indicates that the nature of a message influences the later behaviour of participants, Horowitz (1969) pointed out that the findings of other studies using fear-arousal as a means of changing attitudes have varied considerably, and he maintains that this may be to do with whether the participants are volunteers or not. Horowitz claims that volunteers might appear to be more influenced by fear-arousing messages because they are going to be more sensitive to the expectations of the researchers. They are likely to realise early on that if the research is looking at attitude change, researchers would probably expect the most frightening messages to have the most influence.

The above discussion should give you some idea of how important is the selection of participants when designing research, and how conclusions can be drawn which in fact relate to the characteristics of the participants alone and not to the population under consideration. It is therefore essential to take the participants into consideration when assessing how effective psychological research is as a way of explaining human behaviour.

The key concepts of sampling
- A population should be identified which represents the people about whom the research is being conducted.
- The sample selected should be representative of that population.
- The way the partipants are obtained must always be taken into account when evaluating the results of the research.

In order to evaluate research in terms of the sample used, apply the following questions to the study:

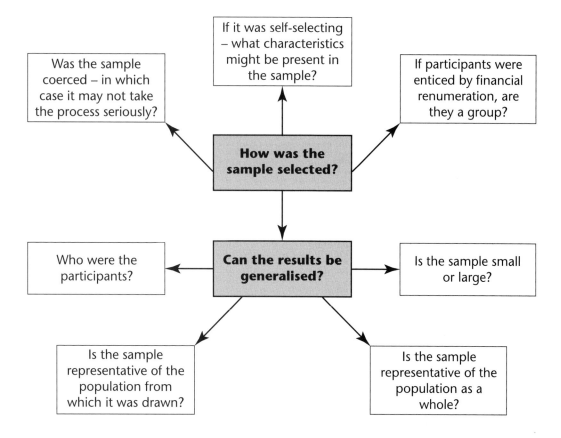

Figure 4.18

More on research methods

5

> *The problems of data collection, measurement and interpretation (including reliability and validity) and the other things to consider along the way*
>
> - *Extraneous or confounding variables*
> - *Demand characteristics*
> - *Experimenter effects*
> - *Experimenter bias*

In this chapter we are going to continue looking at research methodologies. You will have realised by now that in order to evaluate any sort of research, you must try to identify the underlying issues that might affect it. In the last chapter I talked about different methods used by psychologists, many of which I am sure are already familiar to you. Hopefully you are beginning to find many ways of evaluating research from all areas of applied psychology, and the issues we have covered are helping to increase the sophistication of your answers to exam-type questions.

In this chapter I want to talk a little about the idea of actually measuring the performance of participants at various tasks and whether or not the measuring tools are really effective. We are also going to look at the expectations of participants and how these expectations are going to influence the way that they respond.

DATA COLLECTION, MEASUREMENT AND INTERPRETATION

One of the first things a researcher decides is what they want to measure. Certain areas are more easy to measure than others. Simple tests of memory, for instance, can be devised where participants are given something to learn and then, using recognition or recall tests, the amount of information retained can be assessed. The data that is collected is easy to measure – generally speaking, it's either right or wrong. (However, anyone familiar with the work of Bartlett (1939) and Loftus and Palmer, (1974), will recognise that memory may also be *distorted*. But for the sake of argument we will ignore this for the moment.) This means that it is possible to conduct statistical tests and draw conclusions. However, what happens if the researchers intend to measure emotion, attitude, aggression or fear? How can we score something so intangible and subjective?

Asking questions would be one way of getting at these 'feelings', but how useful would someone's descriptions be? Do you think you might misinterpret them (remember experimenter effects)? Here's a way of trying to think about it: What is the colour red like? Is the red I see the same as the red you see? Perhaps I am looking at what you would describe as red but I see it as green and yet I call it red. Is there any way of finding out whether we actually see the same thing? Could we ever find out?

Another question which has caused considerable debate is whether animals see colour in the same way as we do? Many people suggest that animals see only in black and white, although in fact this not true for all animals. One way of investigating this issue is to see whether animals have the same receptors cells at the back of their retinas. Even though they may have what we believe to be the receptors for colour vision, can we ever be sure that these receptor cells work in the same way as ours and that we see colour in the same way? We may assume they do, but at present there is no objective test.

Another example is that of pain measurement. This is studied by **health psychologists** (and is discussed again in some detail in Chapter 7). Think what an abstract concept pain really is. We can't actually measure physically how much pain someone is feeling because it's so subjective and different for all of us.

- We could measure autonomic arousal in terms of blood pressure or heart rate – would this be any good?
- We could ask people directly. But people vary in articulacy – would this be any good?
- We could get them to fill in rating scales – would this be any good?
- We could ask them to colour in pictures with different colours representing different intensities of pain – would this be any good?

Whatever we want to measure must first be carefully defined and converted into some kind of numerical format in order to make comparisons. For instance, we could use some kind of pencil and paper test such as a questionnaire or a rating scale that allows people to transform concepts into scores. Yet if each one of us has a different pain threshold, how can we compare one person's score with another? You must have been in a situation where someone claims to have hurt themselves and you think how pathetic they are. You might just have a higher tolerance of pain than them. If the two of you were to take part in the cold-pressor procedure you might rate the pain as being far lower than the other person. (In this procedure, the participant first immerses his/her arm in a bucket of water at room temperature, then in a bucket of freezing water: see Figure 5.1. Finally, the pain level is rated.) What we really need is a baseline so it would be possible to compare pain levels to assess how bad each of you feels.

A 'baseline' can be provided by getting many people to do the same test. We could use the cold-pressor test, and then look at the average pain rating for holding the arm in water for three minutes. This is known as a standard score and this would then be a three-minute baseline so everyone else's pain could be compared with that. It's a reasonable way of gaining comparisons, but it doesn't get round the possibility that different people might have different sensitivities and their ratings might be more a measure of their stoicism rather than pain intensity.

Data, therefore, is the information gained from the research participants in the study, no matter what the study is investigating. This can be **nominal**, **ordinal** or **interval data**, depending on the design of the study. Obviously interval data is the most 'manipulable' as it can be turned into ordinal data (ranked data) or nominal (categories). Interval data is also the most accurate in providing any sort of measure of central tendency (means, medians and modes) and makes it possible to calculate measures of dispersion (standard deviations) to see the spread of the scores around the mean. This is not simply to enable the researchers to draw lots of pretty graphs, but gives them a better tool to analyse their results and to see if there are trends or idiosyncrasies in the data.

Sometimes it is possible to ignore certain information within the results. Supposing the data contains a 'rogue' score – a score which is really way off the wall and which is influencing all the other results. You have probably noticed that this can happen when you work out the mean score from a set of scores and one person has a result that is way above (or below) that of everyone else. This extreme score will affect the mean score quite dramatically and may make the results look totally different from what was expected. Of course, under normal circumstances, you would notice this immediately. Suppose though, that you were a researcher who found this person's result significant, do you think the researcher is going to look too closely at the individual scores or would he/she be happy to accept them? I am not, for a moment, suggesting that this does happen; after all, results are often checked by more than one person. But it is a possibility.

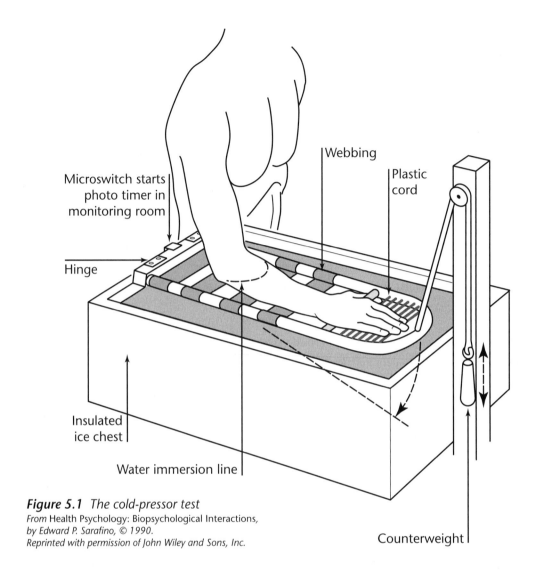

Figure 5.1 *The cold-pressor test*
From Health Psychology: Biopsychological Interactions,
by Edward P. Sarafino, © 1990.
Reprinted with permission of John Wiley and Sons, Inc.

RELIABILITY AND VALIDITY ● ● ● ● ● ● ● ● ● ● ● ● ● ● ● ● ● ●

Having established a definition for research purposes, the investigator still needs to measure the behaviour with an acceptable degree of **validity** and **reliability**. Validity is whether the measuring device is measuring what it is supposed to measure. For example, is a reading test really a measure of intelligence – or simply a measure of reading ability? In this case, we could say that the reading test lacks **construct validity**; it is not measuring the accepted theoretical idea of intelligence which consists of many more abilities besides simply the ability to read.

We can argue that the measures used in some studies may have **face validity**; that is, they *look* as if they are measuring what the researchers wanted to measure –

but they aren't actually addressing the relevant issues. Therefore, when evaluating research, look at the data collected by the researchers and ask yourself if the measurement they have used really is a valid measure of the factor they are investigating.

Perhaps one of the best examples of a measure lacking an element of validity is the measure of aggression. Many studies which have looked at levels of aggression have measured it by either asking participants to administer electric shocks to another person or blasting their eardrums with 'white noise' (a kind of loud static crackling). The shocks or noise are 'given' to confederates of the researcher (stooges) who may or may not have annoyed the participants and, in some cases, who may not even have been seen by the participants.

The following example comes from **environmental psychology.**

> Donnerstein and Wilson (1976) divided a group of subjects in two and used a stooge to make the subjects in one group angry. The researchers then exposed subjects to either 55 dB or 95 dB of unpredictable, one-second noise bursts when they were given the opportunity to (supposedly) administer electric shocks to the stooge. The angered subjects delivered more intense shocks than the non-angered ones and the ones who had received the loudest noise were the most aggressive. However, the noise made no difference to the intensity of shocks for the non-angered group.

Do you think that administering electric shocks to another person really is a valid measure of aggression? If we are measuring acts of aggression, then administering electric shocks to someone has to be considered an aggressive act and therefore a valid measure of aggressive behaviour. However, I seriously doubt that it gets at the real 'core' of aggression; that is, does the person have levels of aggression that are in general higher than the norm or was it only in this instance? Perhaps the participants were simply responding to demand characteristics of the study, or just finding out what it felt like to give another person an electric shock whilst transferring any personal guilt from themselves onto the researcher. Perhaps the participants in this study didn't actually believe they were giving electric shocks. Whatever the beliefs of the participants, perhaps they were simply going along with the requirements of the researchers without actually feeling any aggression at all.

I think I would find it hard to give electric shocks to another person, despite the findings of Milgram. Being a psychologist, I would be very suspicious about the reasons for doing it in the first place. I also think it would be even more difficult if I could see the face of the person I was supposed to be 'shocking', even if they had angered me. In fact a study by Lerner and Lichtman (1968) discovered that people don't seem to be very happy about giving others electric shocks if they know anything about the other person. They found that over 70 per cent of people in one study claimed that they would rather endure the pain themselves than give shocks to another person if they had been told that the other person was 'really scared', although this level decreased to less than ten per cent if they knew nothing about the other person. However, these people had not been 'aroused' and were simply answering questions. Sometimes we can claim we wouldn't act in an aggressive way when we are removed from a situation, but when we are involved, feelings change. Therefore we must remember that Lerner and Lichtman's findings were in response to questioning alone, not a real-life situation. You must bear this in mind when considering whether we can really judge aggresion by looking at the administration of electric shocks in a laboratory environment.

The problem here lies in the fact that we have to identify whether aggression is simply a *feeling* or the *behaviour* that is provoked by the feeling. If we believe it is simply a feeling we can ask our participants to rate how aggressive they feel on a Likert scale, but simply by going through the process of reading the instructions and holding a pen, they may well have calmed down (assuming they were aroused in the first place).

Note: It might be worth mentioning here 'external validity'. External validity is really the same as ecological validity, i.e. the results should be generalisable to the population as a whole at different times and in different places (see Chapter 7).

I would expect that the results from certain pieces of research may well vary slightly over time. After all, society changes and develops and so frequently produces changes in values and beliefs. Therefore if you replicate research that was conducted a number of years ago, you may well find that the results are very different. I always think of Milgram's research when teaching about changes over time. I like to think that we are now far more critical of authority figures and not so likely to obey blindly; this impression is reinforced when students nowadays are more willing to question the reason for having to do certain pieces of work or to behave in certain ways. No longer does the phrase 'Because I said so' seem to be sufficient justification!

If this is the case, do you think it is fair to argue that the results of the original studies were unreliable? Reliability really means consistency; that is, were the results consistent over time and between studies if the same participants were tested? Sometimes a variation from the original results may suggest that there was an error in the measurement and therefore the results were not reliable – like having a fabric tape measure that stretches over time and therefore gives different measurements. However, it is also essential to look at the date research was conducted because it may explain the differing results – perhaps they were reliable when the study was undertaken, but could no longer be considered a reflection of today's behaviour. The study which perhaps best illustrates this is the Hraba and Grant (1970) study which looked at doll preference in black children and found that black children preferred black, rather than white, dolls. The findings were very different from the original study conducted in 1939 by Clark and Clark who found that the black children preferred white dolls. The findings of the original study were probably reliable because it is likely that the same preferences would be made by the participants if the study had been conducted again. In the second study a different set of children was used at a different time. Fisher (1982) suggests that many researchers are unable to replicate studies because of lack of funding, and it seems that journal editors are less than enthusiastic to publish studies which do not demonstrate new effects. Therefore, we often have to speculate about the reliability of research as the supporting evidence is often unavailable.

Figure 5.2 Nowadays children prefer dolls with a corresponding skin colour to their own

Remember that trying to ensure tests are both valid and reliable is especially difficult for basic personality traits such as **assertiveness** or **honesty**, which are very much affected by the situation. This is why snapshot studies (such as that of Piliavin *et al.* (1969)) often miss the basic essence of the participants who respond to the situation rather than the test itself. Another problem is the fact that there is no 'concrete' agreement about what the trait actually is that is being measured. Think of the controversy surrounding the definition of intelligence – there is still no universally accepted definition. It now seems that people's scores on any of the varied IQ tests seem to be sufficient to define the trait, even though the tests may be measuring very different skills.

Before we leave the topic of reliability and validity, there are two studies from **health psychology** that we ought to look at.

McKinstry and Wang (1991) were investigating whether the appearance of a doctor was important to the patients. The researchers showed pictures of doctors to patients attending surgeries. The pictures were of the same male or female doctor dressed either formally (white coat over suit or skirt) or very informally (jeans and open-necked, short-sleeved shirt or pink trousers, jumper and gold earrings.) The patients were asked to rate how happy they would be to consult the doctors in the pictures and how much confidence they would have in their ability. The results showed that the images of traditionally dressed doctors were given higher preference ratings than those who were casually dressed, especially by the older and professional patients.

The results suggested that patients felt more confident with the more traditionally dressed doctors because they fitted into the stereotypical schema of what a doctor should be like.

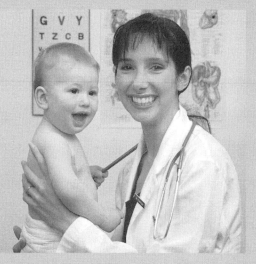

Figure 5.3 *Traditional white coats produce more confidence*

Here participants were asked to rate pictures that had no depth or dimension. If you see a photograph of a person, does this really tell you what the person is like? Although it might give you an initial impression, meeting someone in the flesh can be very different – they may seem warm and friendly or cold and impersonal. I believe that these attributes have far more impact on our impression of someone than the type of clothes they are wearing. Therefore although the study was useful, I believe the results may have lacked an element of validity because rating photos is not the same as rating people – the study was valid as a measure of photo rating, but not necessarily doctor rating!

The other study (which we've already discussed in Chapter 1) looks at how much of the information given by health workers is actually understood, in the belief that this will affect compliance levels. How can you comply with a health request when you don't understand what on earth the doctor is going on about?

McKinlay (1975) conducted an investigation into how much of the information given by health workers to 'lower-class women' in a maternity ward was actually understood. The researchers asked the women if they understood a number of terms, such as 'breech, purgative, protein, mucus, glucose, antibiotic, umbilicus and navel'. The results showed that on average each of the terms was understood by less than 40 per cent of the women although over two-thirds understood 'breech' and 'navel'; interestingly enough almost none understood 'protein' and 'umbilicus'.

At the end of the study, the health workers admitted that they expected only about 40 per cent of their patients to understand the terms. It was concluded that they may have used them out of habit, to patronise, to sound powerful or simply to keep the conversation brief. The patients would be unlikely to ask if they didn't understand the terms for fear of looking stupid.

This is really a study on how to test linguistic knowledge totally out of context; given a list of terms, the women found them difficult to understand, though they may have inferred their meaning in the course of a normal conversation. We often use the context of unfamiliar words to derive their meaning, so how valid is the study as a test of people's understanding of doctors' advice?

Social desirability

Just a quick mention here about the effects of social desirability – the tendency for people to give answers which are more socially acceptable or desirable rather than true. Although this can be very disconcerting for the researcher, it is understandable that it happens. After all, none of us want to be judged unfavourably by another person and, by giving answers that are not socially acceptable, this may happen. Imagine for a moment that you were frequently slapped when you were a child if you did something wrong. Now you are an adult and although you feel that slapping is not really acceptable, you reason that it didn't do you any long-term harm so why shouldn't you, in turn, slap your children when they break the rules? Now imagine that a researcher asks you about your opinions on corporal punishment for children – what would you say? The chances are you would not start going on about how you beat your children at least once a day with the most excellent cane you keep to hand by the side of your dining room table.

Now imagine that someone is trying to assess your personality to find out if you are neurotic or stable. They might ask whether you ever hear voices or shake uncontrollably from time to time. You would probably say 'of course not' because either you would have no idea of what they meant, or you wouldn't want the researcher to think you were a wierdo!

Be aware that if the researcher is investigating some sort of socially sensitive topic, people may lie. This can also happen if people give answers which are intended to try and please the researcher by saying what they think he or she wants them to say. These kind of responses are conforming to demand characteristics, which are discussed in more detail later in the chapter.)

How impressive is the quality of the data?
- Did the researchers effectively define the concept they were interested in?
- Did they successfully convert that concept into a form whereby it could be measured numerically?
- Did the test measure what it was supposed to measure (was it a valid test)?
- Were the measurements reliable?
- Would they have been the same at a different time with different participants?
- Did the participants simply give socially acceptable answers?

EXTRANEOUS AND CONFOUNDING VARIABLES • • • • •

Whenever researchers conduct any sort of study, no matter what kind of methodology they use, there may well be other factors which have not been taken into account, but which may influence or even cause the results (resulting in the study lacking **internal validity** – see Chapter 7). Let's take the example of children's development. Putting children in an unfamiliar environment and getting them to participate in unfamiliar tasks can be an invitation to disaster. The influence of the environment on their behaviour is an **extraneous variable** (or **extra variable**), which you have not taken into account when designing the study. Some children might be so intimidated by the situation that they fail to perform any of the tasks required of them!

Extraneous variables (sometimes known as nuisance variables) are variables that are 'extra' to the ones you are interested in, which may affect the dependent variable (result) of your research. These extra variables may be things like sudden temperature fluctuations or unexpected loud noises or other annoying factors which you cannot anticipate but which would possibly influence the performance of participants. They are most often found in experiments rather than other research although they may occur in observational studies where normal behaviours can be easily disrupted. The thing that differentiates extraneous variables from confounding variables is that they are controllable if they are anticipated. **Order effects** are also examples of extraneous variables, as are **practice** and **fatigue effects**.

If we put a child in its naturalistic environment, it will upset it far less than putting it in a laboratory, but it might also result in more **confounding variables** than the laboratory environment and in turn, these may 'contaminate' the results. This will mean that there can be no certainty as to what caused the responses produced by the child. Confounding variables are variables that may 'confuse' the results – you think they are the result of something you have manipulated when in fact they are actually due to something else. An example would be if you were checking the effectiveness of an education programme that aimed to teach children manual dexterity. You have experimental and control groups of children and use the task of cutting out complicated shapes to illustrate their learned skills. However, you fail to take into account the fact that the majority of children in one group are left-handed and all the scissors are for right-handed people. This variable would confound or confuse the results because the left-handed children would be severely disadvantaged by the tools they were given.

Another example of how a confounding variable can affect the results of research can be found in studies about the nature of leaders. Although it would be possible to ascertain what personality characteristics successful leaders have, it might not necessarily be these that are dictating their success – it might be more to do with the appearance of the person, for instance whether or not they are tall of stature or, more commonly, a combination of several factors.

There are many examples of confounding variables from all areas of applied psychology. A piece of research from the field of **criminal psychology** illustrates how something as easily overlooked as an accent can influence the nature of the response to the guilt of an offender.

> Mahoney and Dixon (1997) played a series of recordings of a two-minute police interview with a suspect, to 119 white non-Birmingham students. They were interested to see whether the accent of a defendant would be likely to influence the number of guilty verdicts of the jury. The recordings were either made in a 'white-Brummie', 'black-Brummie' or 'non-Brummie' accent. Those with 'Brummie' accents were perceived as more guilty than 'non-Brummie', with the 'black-Brummie' being perceived as the most guilty of the three groups.

Bearing in mind that all three groups said identical things, it was the accent alone that influenced the participants to perceive differences in guilt. Now supposing two or three researchers undertake an investigation and each one deals with a different experimental condition – if something as simple as an accent can affect judgements of guilt, then perhaps the behaviour of the researchers will have a tremendous impact on their participants and ultimately cause the effects to occur, rather than the topic under consideration.

Applying Skills to Psychology

The example below from **sports psychology** looks at the influence of audience effects on players.

Michaels *et al.* (1982) arranged for four confederates to watch pool players in a college student union. The games selected to be watched were games which featured both 'above average' and 'below average' players. The researchers found that the players' performance when they didn't know they were being watched was significantly different to their performance when they realised they were being watched. Below average players got worse and above average players got better.

Figure 5.4 Do audiences affect performance in pool games?

The findings were explained by the fact that the players would be aroused although the poor players may have higher arousal levels than the confident players. If an audience arrived, the confident players' arousal levels would take them to the optimum level for good performance whereas if they were not good players then the extra arousal produced by an audience would be enough to take them 'over the top' and produce a performance decrement.

However, perhaps it was the nature of the people watching which produced a performance decrement rather than the simple fact that the students were being watched. Although I am sure that the study aimed to control some of the confounding variables, it may have been the case that the researchers inadvertently stood closer in the 'poor players' condition or perhaps they stood in a place that obscured the light. Perhaps it was simply something more threatening about their behaviour in one condition rather than another which was enough to produce the results.

Another example comes from **health psychology** where people were encouraged to follow a health regime.

Johnson and Johnson began a *Live for Life* programme in 1978. This aimed to encourage as many employees as possible to live healthier lives by informing them of how to improve health, reduce stress, exercise regularly, stop smoking and control their weight. It was considered to be successful when it was evaluated by comparing the health and behaviour of its members with that of employees from different companies who did not have the programme offered to them.

How do we know that other factors were not responsible for either the *Live for Life* brigade's increased health, or the significantly poorer health of the non-participants health? The *Live for Life's* participants' improved health may have been due to the fact that they suddenly felt that their employers actually cared about them. This may in turn have increased their feelings of self-esteem as they came to believe that they were important to their employers. This may have been the trigger to the change in behaviours and not simply the actual campaign itself. After all, if you feel good about yourself you are more likely to take care of yourself and this is part of the battle for good health. Irrespective of how it worked, the campaign was a success!

Has the research been affected by extraneous or confounding variables?
- Was there anything which may have affected the performance or behaviour of the participants sufficiently to change their normal performance, which could have been controlled if it had been anticipated? (*extraneous variables*)
- Was there anything that may have consistently influenced the results besides the independent variable, which the researchers were totally unaware of. Even if they did discover it, would they have been able to do anything about it? (*confounding variables*)

EXPERIMENTER EFFECTS ●

Experimenter effects are where a researcher influences a study in some way. They are caused by experimenter–subject interaction which occurs as a result of the researcher unconsciously influencing the results, either by giving some kind of verbal cue in the way he talks to the different groups of participants, or even in facial expressions or body language.

The most profound experimenter effects can be found in placebo trials. These are drug trials where half the participants are given the drug and the other half receive the placebo (or sugar pill which has no chemical effects). Here researchers who believe strongly in their new drug may give it to participants whilst smiling and sending all sorts of positive messages to them. They may, on the other hand, look disinterested when handing out the sugar pill, knowing it will have no effect and therefore passing this on to the participants.

Coolican (1994) states that between 1968 and 1976, forty experiments failed to find any evidence of experimenter effects but there are other studies which have indicated that it does occur. How prevalent it is in research is debatable, but the most important thing to remember is that it is a possibility and should be considered in any evaluation.

Probably the most well-known example of experimenter effects comes from the study by Rosenthal and his rats.

> Rosenthal and Fode (1963) instructed a group of experimental psychology students that they were to be given experience at conducting an experiment. The study would also give them the chance to become familiar with handling rats and recording data. The students were divided into two groups and were given what they believed were either 'maze-bright' or 'maze-dull' rats. In fact there was no difference between the two groups of rats and they were simply randomly selected from the same stock so the only differences between them were in the minds of the students. The rats were deprived of food prior to the start of the study and then put in a T maze to learn that one 'leg' of the top of the T, which was painted black, would be where the food could be found. The rats were tested on ten occasions every day for five days, with the 'leg' being randomly changed from the left hand top to the right hand top between trials. However food was always found in the black 'leg'.
>
> At the end of the study, the supposedly maze-bright rats achieved significantly more correct choices and these had increased over the five-day period. When the students were asked about their interactions with the rats, not only were the ones who were given the 'bright' rats at the beginning more enthusiastic about their rats but they handled them more, rated them as cleaner, more tame, more intelligent and more pleasant than the 'dull' rats. They also were far more gentle with them than the other group of students.

Here the influence of the students on their 'subjects' made a tremendous difference to how they performed. Their expectations about the rats were translated into the rats' performance. This seems even more impressive than the responses of humans because we are probably far more able to pick up non-verbal cues from each other than are rats. Here you can see how powerful experimenter effects can be. This is why, in drug trials nowadays, the researchers are also kept in the dark about who is receiving the real drug and who is to get the placebo to ensure that their behaviour in no way influences the results.

EXPERIMENTER BIAS ●

You will know if you have done any sort of research, that you want to get significant results; then you can accept your experimental hypothesis. You will have suggested a specific hypothesis because that is the way you believe the results will go. This belief may inadvertently be passed on to the participants in your research (experimenter effects) and therefore influence the participants in the same direction. It is very easy to be a biased experimenter. However, if you stand back and try and look objectively at what you have done, you might question whether that behaviour you observed really was, say, aggressive. You may even have to consider whether the results *really* are significant or are simply an artefact of some other confounding variable.

Psychological research is undertaken by people who are not dissimilar to you – so they too may see what they want to see, or find what they want to find. They might then misinterpret their data accordingly, and no one would be any the wiser. In fact, they may even fool themselves.

> **Has the research been influenced by experimenter effects?**
> * Has the researcher influenced his participants in some way, for example, by the tone of his voice or his facial expression?
> * Do you think the researcher has actually interpreted his data in a biased way as a means of supporting his hypothesis?
> * Has he overlooked any other possible explanation for the results?

DEMAND CHARACTERISTICS ●

On occasions, participants try to work out what the study is about and this may influence their behaviour. They may wish to please the researcher by doing what they think he expects them to do, rather than what they would naturally do. Obviously this is going to make the results inaccurate. This kind of behaviour is known as conforming to **demand characteristics**. (The section in Chapter 5 on 'participants' looks at what kind of person is most likely to conform to demand characteristics.)

Demand characteristics are features of the experimental situation that cause participants to act in a certain way, in the belief that this is required from them.

Martin Orne, who died in 2000, is well known for conducting research illustrating the effect of demand characteristics on participant behaviour. He demonstrated in a number of studies that people behave very differently in a psychological study to the way they behave in everyday life. In one study he asked a number of people whether they would carry out five push-ups as a personal favour and, not surprisingly, they all refused. However, when he played the role of research psychologist, they were all willing to help, presumably believing in the value of such research to our overall psychological knowledge.

I demonstrated this to a new psychology class fairly recently. I told the students that we were going to do a practical and that I needed a volunteer. After they had all looked around at each other wondering what dastardly deed I was going to involve them in, one student volunteered. I asked him to go outside the classroom and stand by a tree on the lawn in front of my room and when he got there, he was to jump up and down while he counted to twenty-five. When he returned I fully debriefed him and explained the purpose of my instructions which was to demonstrate the concept of demand characteristics. He explained that as I had said we were going to have a practical lesson, he thought he must be demonstrating some kind of serious psychological concept (which he was), although it was not one that he had in mind! I tried the same trick with a different student from another class later that day but the only difference was that I didn't say that it was part of a practical demonstration. The only response I got in this case was 'You must be joking!'.

In one study Orne (1959) showed how the behaviour of participants was affected by knowledge gained earlier outside the laboratory. He (1959) demonstrated this phenomenon by presenting false information to college students when he was giving them a lecture about hypnosis. He talked about a strange characteristic that occurred when people entered a hypnotised state, claiming that they demonstrated 'catalepsy of the dominant hand'. This meant that if they were, say, right handed, their hand would take on a waxen flexibility or rigidity, and he demonstrated this to his audience by using 'stooges'. Orne also set up a control group of students who had the same lecture without the mention of the hand-catalepsy.

Some weeks later Orne invited all the students to take part in a hypnosis study which involved being hypnotised. He found that when they were hypnotised, most of the students who had seen the hand-catalepsy demonstrated it whilst it was absent in the entire control group. The experimental group were therefore 'behaving' in the way they thought they should behave by demonstrating demand characteristics.

If this is the case for such a study where the students had received prior information about the way they should behave, it makes sense to think that the majority of participants will behave in what they see as the required way. However, it is not always obvious what the required way is, as demonstrated by Orne (1962) when he was investigating whether subjects who were hypnotised were more obedient.

Before he started the study, he took away the participants' watches. He then asked them to add up rows of numbers on sheets filled with randomly generated numbers. Each subject was given 2000 sheets and each sheet meant they would have to make 224 calculations. He told them to continue to work and that he was leaving the room but would be back later. To his amazement they were still working after five-and-a-half hours. To ensure that the results weren't simply due to obedience to a visible authority figure, he decided to remove himself from the experiment. Once they had finished a sheet, they were to pick up a card from a pile that would tell them what to do next. The card said 'You are to tear up the sheet of paper which you have just completed into a minimum of 32 pieces and go on to the next sheet of paper and continue working as you did before. When you have completed this piece of paper, pick up the next card which will instruct you further. Work as accurately and rapidly as you can'.

Again the participants continued to work for prolonged periods of time, believing that the study was extremely relevant.

We must therefore remember that participants are not naïve and unintelligent but need to have some kind of information as to what a study is about. If that information is not forthcoming, they will 'invent' some kind of rationale or explanation about the study and this in turn can influence their behaviour.

> **The key features of demand characteristics**
> * Participants may try to please the researcher by doing what they think they should do according to their interpretation of the study.
> * Participants may try to upset the research by acting in the *opposite* way to the way they think they should, according to their interpretation of the study.

So where does this leave us in terms of evaluation? What we need to do is to evaluate studies in terms of the type of data that was collected and look at whether the measurement of that particular concept was really valid. We also need to know whether the researcher inadvertently influenced his participants and whether they tried to work out what he wanted them to do.

In order to evaluate research in terms of data collection, measurement and interpretation, apply the questions on the next page to the study.

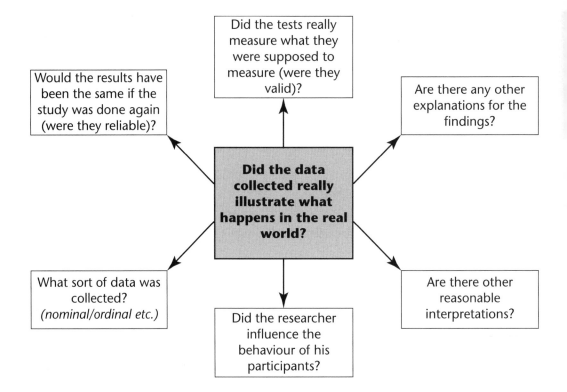

Figure 5.5

Ethics

6

> **The history of ethical guidelines and the current BPS code.**
>
> - **Consent**
> - **Deception**
> - **Debriefing**
> - **Withdrawal**
> - **Privacy**
> - **Protection of participants**
> - **Observations**

When students are asked to undertake a piece of research, teachers always encourage them to make sure their research conforms to ethical guidelines. For example, research which involves looking at the effects of alcohol on performance using a sample of 16-year-old students, who are asked to drink about eight vodkas and orange, then walk across a tightrope with no safety net, is actually unethical (although it may be amusing to watch). But who decides it's unethical and what happens if you do carry out just such a piece of research?

A BRIEF HISTORY OF ETHICAL GUIDELINES ● ● ● ● ● ● ● ●

A great deal of the research done in the early 1960s did not take into account a number of issues which we consider today are very much fundamental to human rights. It isn't correct to assume that there were no ethical guidelines in existence at that time. In fact the first moves to consider ethics in psychology date back to 1938 when the American Psychological Association (APA) formed a committee to investigate whether it was a good idea to draft an ethical code for psychologists. However, it was not until 1947 that work began on a written set of guidelines which went through a number of revision and modification processes until they were finally approved by the APA in 1953.

The impetus for this set of guidelines was the fascination with psychometric testing which had started during the war. In fact, as Gould's (1982) article illustrates, the status of psychology had increased during the First World War when the idea of intelligence testing had been accepted as an accurate measure of the innate intelligence of would-be soldiers, and this belief in the usefulness of intelligence testing for military placements such as espionage or intelligence missions continued during the Second World War. In fact I expect if I asked you if you would like to know your IQ and your personality type, you would willingly agree to take the tests because you want to know what you are and how intelligent you are compared with others. The problems with this speak for themselves. If I said to you that I am willing to give you the relevant tests but only if I can make your results known to the rest of your family and friends, you may be less willing because you might feel that they would judge you. If, on the other hand, you did the tests and only you knew the answers, it might be a very different matter.

It was just such a situation that resulted in the need for ethical guidelines covering personal privacy, confidentiality and the prevention of those results being misused. Only four of the 171 pages in the 1953 standards actually related directly to the use of human participants in research. The other 167 pages focused on more generalised areas of research, teaching and professional practice; however, it was a start! The trouble was that researchers largely ignored the original guidelines because they were very generalised and really more or less unenforceable (Vinacke, 1954).

It was not until 1971, after some controversial research undertaken by Milgram and Zimbardo, that the need to re-evaluate the ethical guidelines was addressed. In 1973 the first code of conduct for human participants was published containing ten research principles, which were intended to protect the welfare of humans involved in research. For someone who still finds it hard to get out of the habit of calling participants 'subjects' (a habit I acquired at university), I was interested to note that these 1973 principles changed the way in which we should refer to people involved in research. The guidelines stated that people involved in research should be known as 'participants' rather than 'subjects', and 'experimenters' should be known as 'researchers', presumably as a way of distancing research from the more gruesome idea of subjecting our participants to our wicked experimental designs!

I was surprised to discover that the British Psychological Society didn't produce their *Ethical Principles* for human participants until 1978, which was subsequently revised in 1985 and again in 1995. It seemed quite late to me, bearing in mind that psychology was increasing in status as the years went by. On the other hand, the British Society was the first to put in place a separate list of ethical guidelines to protect the welfare of animals in psychological research. Other countries have their own codes of ethics which all seem to have as their focus the underlying principle of respect for human beings, and cover issues such as informed consent and the welfare of participants. I must admit, I had always assumed that all countries abided by the same set of guidelines, and was quite surprised to find all the different organisations had slightly different codes of practice.

We will now have a look at the ethical guidelines which apply to the British Psychological Society. Of course these guidelines are the latest, and it is acceptable to look at past research on the basis of how ethical it was using these current guidelines. However, it is not always fair to judge researchers in the past as being cruel and harsh because of the lack of understanding of ethical principles. We must remember that they were simply carrying out research deemed acceptable at the time and, it could be argued, were in a state of 'blissful ignorance' of how they were to be judged in future years. We must also remember that one of the important issues in any research (past or present) is the balance between the need to conform to ethical guidelines and the value of the subsequent findings. This does not exonerate blatant breaches of ethical guidelines, but when the boundaries are 'grey' it may influence how you judge research.

THE MAIN PRINCIPLES OF THE BRITISH PSYCHOLOGICAL SOCIETY'S 'ETHICAL GUIDELINES' FOR PSYCHOLOGICAL RESEARCH (1995) ● ● ● ● ● ● ● ● ●

The guidelines stress that any research should be objective, competent and non-wasteful. This makes total sense if we are to consider psychology as a scientific discipline.

- What the guidelines are trying to ensure is that the results of psychological research should be interpreted in an objective way rather than be 'moulded' to fit the ideas of the researcher in order to back up their ideas and beliefs.
- The research should be carried out in a competent way so that the findings can be accepted as being valid and reliable and if necessary, the work could be replicated at a later date.
- The research should be 'non-wasteful' which means that it should not be carried out simply 'for fun' but should be used to investigate a specific topic and be documented accordingly. The data provided by participants should not be discarded if it does not fit in with the expectations of the researcher, so their efforts should not be considered to be inconsequential.

- Finally, psychologists are responsible for making sure that any data and findings from their research are available for public inspection, but this information must not be misinterpreted or abused.

Therefore we must consider the following:

The **consent** of participants should be obtained wherever possible. This should ideally be **informed consent** where the researchers explain, as fully as possible, the purpose and design of the research. If the research involves children who are too young to give consent, that consent must be given by the child's caregiver or person responsible for that child.

Participants should not be **deceived** about the nature of the research if this is possible, although on occasion it is necessary.

At the end of the research process, the investigator should **debrief** the participants by explaining to them the nature of the research. They should also discuss the procedure and answer any further questions, their intention being to make sure that **the participants leave the research situation, as far as possible, in the state in which they entered**. Participants who feel unhappy about the situation after they have been debriefed can have their data withdrawn and destroyed in their presence.

Researchers must tell their participants that they have a right to **withdraw**, without penalty, at any stage of the research.

Any information provided by participants must be treated **confidentially** and the researchers must ensure that their identities will not be revealed unless they have given prior informed consent. (The Data Protection Act makes this a legal requirement.)

All participants must be protected from mental or physical harm during the investigation so they must not be put in a situation of greater **risk** than they would encounter in their everyday life.

If the research involves observation and the participants have not given their informed consent, the **observations** should only take place in situations where people would normally expect to be in public view.

The ethical guidelines make sense if we consider that psychology is aimed at understanding human beings' minds and behaviour – presumably with the intention of safeguarding and maintaining their welfare in the future. Could we really justify research if it involved *intentionally* harming individuals in the name of science?

What happens if research is deemed unethical?

We have a problem here because before the guidelines were laid down research was undertaken at the discretion of the researchers. Even Milgram claimed that he had not expected his results and had done his utmost to ensure the participants suffered no long-term consequences by debriefing them and by checking them out a year later. However, Milgram was seen as the 'wicked wizard' of psychological research by a number of authors, because he did not allow his participants to withdraw and subjected them to considerably more stress than they would have experienced in everyday life. Yet can we blame Milgram totally? He was not subjected to the same rules of conduct that are in existence today because at that time they didn't exist, so he didn't actually break them. Therefore, what we have to do is to say that by today's standards Milgram's research was unethical. (Perhaps, with hindsight, he might have been a little less insistent with his participants – but then surely this research was about obedience so he could hardly have turned round to them and said 'You must continue, you must go on – but if you really don't want to – you can leave!')

If a researcher blatantly ignores ethical guidelines, what penalties would he/she incur? And would the results of that research be ignored? We have to remember that codes are obligations to behave in a certain way – they put the onus on the shoulders of the researcher by making him/her personally accountable. Therefore, theoretically, should a researcher ignore ethical guidelines, they are in danger of being 'struck off' and having their membership of the BPS cancelled, and their research would not be published by any reputable journal. However, what real censure is this? (I am sure a tabloid newspaper would be more than willing to print the findings and probably pay very well for the privilege.)

ETHICS AS AN EVALUATIVE ISSUE IN ESSAY WRITING

Having been through the issues of ethical guidelines, let's consider some research and look at how it breaches the code of ethics we now accept. From these examples, I hope to give you an idea of how to address the issue of ethics when discussing weaknesses in psychological research.

Did the participants give their consent?

Although ethical guidelines state that we should have informed consent from participants when carrying out research, do you think this is always necessary? What happens if the procedure is unlikely to have any effect on participants' lives and won't put them at any sort of risk – is it really necessary in cases like this to gain their informed consent? This is even more relevant if, by giving their informed consent, they will change their responses to our research making our findings unrepresentative of the norm. What makes the situation worse is that when research is undertaken in a field setting, sometimes it isn't possible to get participants' consent, let alone their informed consent. Are we seriously breaking ethical guidelines?

What you have to decide as the evaluator of the research, is whether researchers are really breaking ethical guidelines. It is quite acceptable to look at research and conclude that in an ideal world consent should have been given, but that in this instance it was impossible/counterproductive to the findings or not really necessary.

Let me give you some examples of research which involve these situations.

Stress has been known to negatively affect performance and in order to investigate this, specifically in a military situation, United States Army scientists undertook a series of experiments in the 1960s. In order to make the stress authentic, the army recruits who were the subjects in this research were involved in cleverly organised and elaborate hoax situations and therefore did not give their informed consent.

One study involved 66 recruits who were undergoing basic training aboard a military aircraft. Their stress was manipulated by witnessing one of the propellers situated on the wing actually stop turning, followed by a conversation over the intercom that described further malfunctions of the plane. They were then told that the plane was about to crash-land and this was supported further by an invented conversation between the air traffic controllers and the sight of ambulances and fire trucks on the landing strip.

The recruits were then given an extremely complicated questionnaire asking about how they wanted their personal possessions disposed of in the case of death and a multiple choice questionnaire to find out how much they remembered of airborne emergency procedures to give to the army's insurance company. (The recruits were told that these documents would be put in an indestructible container and ejected before the crash.)

When the plan finally landed (safely), the subjects were told that the whole procedure was part of a research investigation and they had blood and urine samples taken for evidence of stress levels.

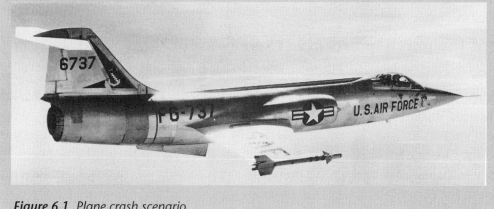

Figure 6.1 Plane crash scenario

How do you feel about such a study – was it justified? If we were evaluating it for breaches of ethical guidelines, it would breach more than simply informed consent. However, we must remember that there were no specific guidelines in existence in the 1960s, although the levels of stress suffered by the participants were excessive to say the least. We could also argue in defence of the study, that they had joined a military force which would involve them in risk of life, so in effect the researchers had not subjected them to greater risk than they might be subjected to in their everyday lives. The other issue is, how else could you produce such 'ecologically valid' stress of that magnitude with subjects giving their consent? Even if they were unaware of the actual procedure, simply the knowledge that they were taking part in an experiment of some kind would be sufficient to suggest the 'plane crash scenario' was fiction!

Now let's consider a study which is far less obvious taken from environmental psychology.

> Barefoot *et al.* (1972) were investigating how difficult it is to invade someone's personal space. They put a lone confederate at three different distances from a public drinking fountain. The confederate stood either one foot, five feet or ten feet from the drinking fountain and the researchers watched what happened next. It was found that very few passers-by approached the fountain when the confederate was standing one foot away, but more were willing to approach with the increasing distance of the confederate. They also discovered that when the area was crowded, people had few problems in invading the confederate's personal space.

The participants in this study had no idea that they were taking part in psychological research, therefore they did not give their consent. Is this an ethical piece of research?

According to the ethical guidelines, it *has* ignored the issue of consent *but* we have to consider whether the 'participants' were damaged in any way by the research, and if it really was necessary to involve them in knowing that their normal behaviour had been observed and had been noted. I think in a case like this, they might be more upset if they knew they had been watched than if they had been left in blissful ignorance. If I were evaluating this study as part of an examination question, these are the points I would make. Too often students fail to think about ethical issues on a practical basis – the people were in a public place and were simply doing what came naturally and they were not being identified, so where is the harm?

The next study, again taken from environmental psychology, also failed to get informed consent from the participants.

> Ruback and Pandey (1992) were interested in the attitudes of passengers of three-wheeled motorised 'Tuk tuks' which are used as taxis in India and South-east Asia. The passengers' attitudes and behaviour reflected the level of crowding and temperature, with hotter and more crowded environments producing poorer attitudes and more anti-social behaviour. However, their attitudes were less extreme when warned in advance about the conditions on the roads.

You can see from the final part of the study that actually telling them about the condition on the roads changed their attitudes. This gives you evidence of how important it can be not to affect your participants' responses by gaining informed consent.

Let's look again at the study from the area of health psychology that we first looked at in Chapter 1, this time looking at ethical implications.

> Robinson and West conducted a study in 1992 looking at reasons for the reluctance of patients to disclose their symptoms. They were interested in the amount of information people gave when they attended a genito-urinary clinic (specialising in sexually transmitted diseases). Before they saw the doctor, they were asked to record intimate details of symptoms, previous attendances and sexual behaviour on a questionnaire, which was either written, or on a computer. It was found that people give more significant information to the computer than they give on a written questionnaire.

Once again, the participants had not given their consent to take part in research and yet information provided by them was used to investigate the topic. Look at the date of the study – the guidelines were in existence. Look at the nature of the situation, the participants were deceived. If they had been told they were taking part in a piece of research, do you think they would have willingly taken part, bearing in mind that their answers would have to be closely scrutinised in order to compare them with the level of information given by other participants?

Finally, it is worthwhile thinking about whether participants who are asked if they mind taking part in a study on such and such, really do give informed consent. I have been in a situation before now where I have agreed to take part in some kind of survey, either over the telephone or when someone calls at the door. Why do I agree to it? I suppose I feel sorry for the person whose job it is to get people to take part as I have been in that situation myself. I have been told what the survey is about – consumer knowledge of health issues relating to available products – and I agree to go for it. Half an hour later we have gone off into the realms of insurance or hospital provisions and I am now wishing I hadn't agreed to take part. It turns out that the survey is about health care provision (i.e. private health insurance) rather than buying things from shops and knowing whether they are going to make me healthy or not. I had given informed consent to take part, but I didn't really understand what the whole thing was about because I wasn't really listening. Do you think this could be the same for many of the participants in research: they think they know what's going on and therefore don't bother to pay attention to the explanation, and the researcher doesn't bother to check that they really understand.

Were participants deceived about the study?

Most participants will have experienced some level of deception while taking part in research. The main reason for it is that if they do know exactly what is going on, it is bound to affect their responses due to demand characteristics. Researchers have to assume that the participants are relatively naïve (which is not always the case, especially with psychology students as participants). They also have to assume that in order to be really effective in their deception, the procedure doesn't give away any sort of clues as to what it is all about.

If the conditions provided as a backdrop to a piece of research seem unreal to the participants, then they will not take the research seriously. In fact it is necessary to evaluate research by looking at how realistic it is in terms of mundane and experimental realism (see Chapter 4). Therefore deception is often essential to some degree in order to reduce many of the other effects which seem to haunt psychological research.

Furthermore, it is often difficult to work out how much participants have actually been deceived. Orne (1959) talks about a 'pact of ignorance' that can develop between the researcher and the participant whereby both know that the other knows that they aren't actually being deceived, but they just keep quiet about it rather than invalidate the research.

It has been suggested that one way to get around the problem of deception is to thoroughly debrief participants. Whether this makes up for the initial deception is a different matter but under most circumstances, deception is not really harmful.

There are instances where blatant deception is an essential part of research, such as placebo studies. (Placebos are inert substances like saline, which have no therapeutic effect.) If you are testing the effectiveness of a drug in comparison to a control, you must be careful not to inform the participant which group they are in, otherwise their beliefs may influence their responses. In the following case, the deception is essential in order to assess the drug's real effectiveness. This example comes from the area of health psychology and is a piece of research which investigated the placebo effect on pain. It aimed to find out whether placebos trigger the release of endogenous opioids, which are naturally occurring painkiller biochemicals. These endogenous opioids are produced within the body and are responsible for the inhibition of the transmission of pain signals. Without deception, the research would be impossible.

Levine, Gordon and Fields (1978) looked at a volunteer sample of dental patients who had impacted wisdom teeth removed. They all received nitrous oxide anaesthetic at the start of the surgery which is the painkilling gas often given to women while they are in labour. Two hours later they were given an injection and then they received a further injection after three hours.

The injections contained either naloxone (a substance which prevents the painkilling effects of any kind of opiate) or a placebo and the subjects were told that the injections might increase, decrease or have no effect on the pain. The injections were actually randomly assigned and the technique used was a double blind technique, whereby neither the participants nor the researcher knew which substance was being given.

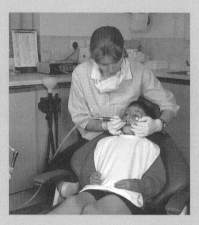

Figure 6.2 *Is it ethical not to give painkillers?*

- One group got the placebo first and then naloxone second.
- One group got naloxone first and then the placebo second.
- The last group were given placebos on both occasions.

The participants were asked to rate the intensity of pain several times during the study. The results were as follows:

- The first group reported more pain when given naloxone than when given the placebo.
- The subjects who got the placebo first and claimed it reduced pain, reported increased pain with naloxone, but the ones who reported no change in pain with the placebo showed no change with the naloxone.

This indicates that the subjects who experienced pain relief with the placebo were actually producing endogenous opioids.

Do you think that this study was unethical? Certainly the subjects were deceived, so according to ethical guidelines it was an unethical study, but it would have been impossible to gain any meaningful results without such deception. The findings also have considerable implications in terms of really evaluating the effectiveness of different drugs.

Another example from the area of **health psychology** is the work of Diane Ruble (1977) who was looking at the perceived severity of symptoms. The suggestion was that premenstrual symptoms would be perceived as more significant if the participant believed she was closer to beginning menstruation.

> Diane Ruble was interested in the role of cognitive factors in symptom perception. She gave women a psychological test which was supposed to accurately pinpoint the timing of the next menstruation. The test could not actually do that but she gave the women feedback that they were either within a couple of days of starting or at least a week away (they were all actually about a week away). All the women then filled out a questionnaire about their symptoms and the ones that thought they were nearer starting gave more symptoms than the others. This indicated that premenstrual symptoms have two component parts, the actual physical responses of the body and the beliefs as to what those responses might be.

In this study, deception was essential, and it is unlikely that it damaged the participants in any way.

Were the participants debriefed or left to go about the rest of their lives having been irreparably harmed?

Of course the most famous study which broke ethical guidelines, insofar as the poor participant never returned to the state in which he entered the research, was 'Little Albert', the small boy who probably spent his life terrified of white rats and other white hairy things (Watson and Rayner, 1920).

Much of the observational research which has been conducted has not included any kind of debriefing and yet the participants, who did not even know they were taking part in research were completely unharmed by the data they provided. There are other studies, however, which have involved systematically manipulating the performance of participants by changing their self-efficacy beliefs, but due to the nature of the participants, debriefing was not considered necessary. One such study comes from the area of educational psychology.

> Hurlock (1925) was interested in the effects of feedback on the behaviour of school children. Hurlock divided a group of ten-year-olds into four groups and gave each group feedback on their performance at solving difficult maths tests. On the first day, three of the groups were given feedback within earshot of each other while the fourth group (the control group), who had been kept separate from the others, received no feedback about their performance. The first of the three groups kept together were told that they had done very well, regardless of how well they did in

reality. The second group was told off for being careless and making lots of mistakes. The third group was ignored although they had heard the comments made to the other two groups. In fact, the performance of all four groups was similar.

Figure 6.3 *How do children respond to feedback?*

However, after the first day, the praised group's work was significantly better than that of the other groups and they were consistently good throughout the whole five days of the study. The group that had been told off improved for a couple of days but then their performance declined. The ignored group performed at a consistently lower level than the group that had been told off, for the whole period of the study. The control group performed worst of all over the whole period.

The conclusions of the study were that some kind of feedback is more effective than none at all, but that positive feedback or reinforcement has a more positive effect on future performance – a kind of self-fulfilling prophecy.

Look at the date of this study – 1925 – before any sort of ethical guidelines had been stipulated. Now think what the children in the study actually felt like and how it influenced their performance. The necessity to debrief them was not an issue at the time, and even if they were debriefed, would they have really understood what was going on? I think that in the short term this study may have affected the children and for that reason it is unethical. They should really have been given another manipulated task to return their self-esteem to normal.

In fact, the issue of whether debriefing really is sufficient to remove any negative consequences of having taken part in research, remains an unanswerable question. Any sort of experience must change us in some way or another and even if we have that experience explained in a different way, we are quite likely to remember the initial feeling when recalling that memory in the future. Therefore debriefing shouldn't be relied on to get rid of any negative consequences. It's not acceptable to suggest that unethical research is really fine because the ethical issues were solved by 'a good old debriefing session'.

Were the participants given the right to withdraw?

Milgram's studies of obedience are most often cited as an example of experiments where participants were not given the opportunity to withdraw. Actually, this isn't correct. Some participants did choose to stop during the procedure – after all you can't actually make a participant continue with the experiment if they decide they no longer want to take part. However, it is rare for research participants to be told that it is quite acceptable for them to leave during the course of the study. How many times have you actually told your participants that they can withdraw if they want to? Probably never, because if they do decide to leave half way through the proceedings, it is a waste of your time and energy and probably means you need to go and find a replacement.

Finding examples of research that have either explicitly allowed or forbidden participants to leave is quite difficult. After all, if participants chose to leave you are unlikely to have been told about it. On the other hand, how likely is it for researchers to enquire at the end of the procedure whether the participants would have liked to give up half-way through? How would they know they could leave if they had not given their consent to participate in the first place?

As you can see, this area of ethics is more a theoretical construct – a good theory but it doesn't often happen in practice. However, many pieces of research which have broken other ethical guidelines due to deception have been guilty in this area.

Was the identity of the participants and the data they provided kept confidential?

Research tends to refer to the participants merely in terms of numbers rather than as individuals. The occasional study will use the initials of the person concerned, for example research into memory might involve individuals such as KF and HB. Specific case studies may also use the person's name, such as 'Clive Wearing', although these instances are few and far between. One area where names are often used is in case studies into famous criminals such as Jeffrey Dahmer, Ian Brady, Myra Hindley (see Figure 6.4) and the Wests. However, this information is in the public domain in any event, due to excessive reporting from the press, and so the reporting of such case histories do not break ethical guidelines in the same way.

It is unlikely that you will ever be able to identify the participants of research and put the data they provided together, but sometimes the researchers themselves

Figure 6.4 *Few of us will be unfamiliar with this image of Myra Hindley. Though there is an ethical need to keep identities in case studies confidential, some cases have been so widely publicised that this can no longer apply*

obtain data to which they really should have no access. I am thinking again here about research within the field of health psychology where information given in confidence to doctors is later analysed by researchers to find out the quality and quantity of that information.

> Roter and Hall (1987) investigated the differing abilities of doctors to get information from their patients. They found that patients were more willing to give doctors diagnostic facts if the doctors asked more questions, gave more information about the cause and prognosis of their patient's illness and talked about prevention and treatment.

Here the information given would have to be looked at carefully in order to come up with some mathematical measure of information. Surely this in itself breaks the guideline of confidentiality, both by the doctors and also by the researchers who had access to confidential information.

Were participants subjected to unnecessary risk?

Few studies subject participants to unnecessary risk. I know of no study which has actually asked participants to walk across tightropes when under the influence of alcohol, or of any other equally worrying design. However, this particular study from the area of health psychology was seriously ethically flawed.

> It has been known for some time that stress can produce or aggravate an asthmatic attack. Studies have shown that suggestion can also induce symptoms in asthmatic subjects, such as the study by Luparello, Lyons, Bleecker and Mcfadden (1968). Asthmatic subjects were required to inhale several doses of a solution which they believed to contain an allergen. Each successive dose was supposed to contain a stronger and stronger dose. Nearly half the subjects developed asthmatic symptoms ranging from relatively mild, in the form of spasms of the bronchial muscles, to full asthmatic attacks.

Obviously it was essential here to deceive the participants in order to test the placebo effect, but asthma can actually be fatal. In fact in the USA, over 5,000 asthmatics die every year. Do you think that the participants in this research were subjected to unnecessary risk? (Look at the date of the research.)

Is an observational study ethical?

I mentioned earlier that observations are acceptable if they are conducted in a place where people would normally be on public display such as by drinking fountains (Barefoot *et al.*, 1972), shopping centres or underground trains. What happens if they are observed in a situation where they would not normally expect to be observed?

One study which immediately springs to mind is the study taken from the area of environmental psychology, which was investigating how invasions of personal space influence arousal.

> Research into personal space suggests that infringement leads to high levels of stress which in turn delays the onset of urination and shortens its duration. Middlemist *et al.* (1976) conducted a study in a 'three urinal' men's lavatory and investigated the topic of personal space. The researchers investigated this phenomenon by one researcher stationing himself in a nearby toilet stall with a 'periscope' hidden in a pile of books on the floor. Using two stopwatches he recorded how long it took before the visitors to the urinal started to urinate and how long they actually urinated for. The level of stress was manipulated by the presence of one or

two others at the urinal and the findings indicated that close interpersonal distances increased the delay and decreased the persistence of urination.

Figure 6.5

The ethics of this study certainly leave a great deal to be desired! Here not only were the participants not consenting to take part in the study but they were also being observed in a place where they would not expect to be observed. They were also unlikely to have been debriefed – 'Excuse me sir, we have just filmed you having a wee!' … You can imagine the response. Here you could legitimately have a field day with regard to ethics although again it would be worth pointing out that the study could not have been done with informed consent. I just question how useful this study really is because I am sure we would all be quite happy to accept that trying to urinate with others present is hard enough. Memories of my nursing days spring to mind with images of ladies perched on bedpans and nurses running taps to try and get them going … Trying to do it with others standing by us is obviously going to make it even more uncomfortable and embarrassing. Do we really need to investigate this phenomenon and wouldn't a questionnaire work just as well?

IN CONCLUSION ●

It is inevitable that some studies will have a 'problem' or two! I may disagree with you regarding the extent of the problem. However, that is fine as long as you have given adequate reasons for your views. At the end of the day, we are all entitled to our own opinions and as long as we can reasonably justify them, that is all that matters.

Also, the kind of arguments I have used should make it obvious that I have actually thought about the research. One way that students lose marks in examinations is by simply producing a list of evaluative issues which read like a shopping list when it is obvious that they haven't really thought about what they are writing.

If we look at a study taken from sports psychology which investigated self-efficacy we can see how it is possible to produce a really poor set of evaluation statements.

> Weinberg *et al.* (1979) asked participants to test their leg strength using a machine which gave false feedback. By giving incorrect feedback they were able to manipulate the participants' beliefs in their own abilities (their sense of self-efficacy). They were then asked to take part in a muscular endurance task which involved sitting down while holding their legs in a horizontal position for as long as possible. The participants who had been given a sense of low self-efficacy did less well than the high self-efficacy subjects.

Example of 'dodgy' evaluation

Study A isn't very good because the participants didn't give informed consent; they were observed by researchers when they didn't think they were being observed but just thought it was part of a PE lesson. They weren't allowed to leave and they might have been permanently affected by the research as they believed they were useless and this might have had long-term consequences. They might have suffered deep vein thrombosis afterwards because of holding their legs up and also it might have hurt. They could have been scarred for life and thought they were useless at everything and they might not have been debriefed. Their data was used without their consent and it could have been possible to work out who the participants were, especially the really useless one who didn't manage to hold his leg up for more than two minutes!

Why is this evaluation dodgy?

The first point is reasonable – the participants may well have agreed to take part in some sort of study to test leg strength, so they gave their consent but they were deceived as to the nature of the study itself. However, if they had given informed consent, the study would not have been effective because participants would have known that the feedback was false and therefore bore no relationship to their real abilities; their self-efficacy could not have been manipulated. If they were asked to take part in a muscular endurance task, they would have had the opportunity to decline. Again, if they gave their consent, it would not be informed consent. Because the test was looking at their ability to hold their legs in a horizontal position for as long as possible, they could not have continued longer than was bearable, and as the researchers were simply timing them, they would not have interfered with the participants' choice to lower their legs. We are not told whether the researchers actually debriefed the participants at the end of the study. If they did, then it is unlikely that they would have suffered any long-term consequences from their efforts because they would have realised that the researchers manipulated their beliefs about their own ability. However, if they failed to debrief them, the participants were unlikely to suffer long-term consequences anyway, and would more likely have simply tried harder next time. The results may even have acted as some kind of future motivation.

In order to evaluate research in terms of ethical considerations, apply the following questions to the study:

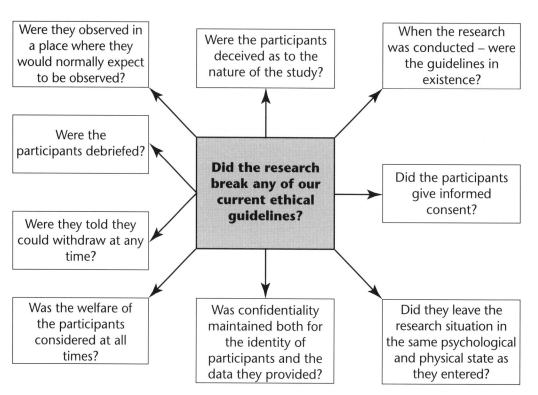

Figure 6.6

Ethnocentrism and all that

7

- **Ethnocentrism**
- **Cultural relativity**
- **Ecological validity**
- **How recent is the research?**
- **Subject variables**

So far we have looked at a number of specific areas that can be used to evaluate psychological research. However, there are some issues which have a much broader basis such as the ethnocentricity of researchers, the ecological validity of their work and when it was carried out. We must also bear in mind the individual differences of the research participants – how each one of us varies in terms of our past experiences, both within our families and within our cultures, and any potential genetic influences on our behaviour.

ETHNOCENTRICITY ●

Have you noticed who seems to be responsible for conducting a vast amount of psychological research? It appears that American psychologists are responsible for much of the research undertaken during the 1960s and 1970s. If you look at the most famous social psychological studies, you will find that they were conducted in America, using as their participants white, American, middle-class undergraduate students who, as you will immediately realise, are hardly representative of the population as a whole. In fact they are really hardly representative of anyone other than white, American, middle class students. To emphasise this point further, in the area of **environmental psychology**, most of the published research tends to be American and was conducted during the 1970s. This does not mean that this was the only research that was being undertaken, however. In fact, there are huge amounts of research that have been conducted but have never been reported or published in textbooks, so the majority of us are unaware of its existence.

So why is it that these pieces of research have been so important in shaping psychological theory? One simple answer to this is that many of the topics that were investigated were being looked at for the first time. The lack of ethical guidelines made it possible for the research to move into new areas that had never been researched before, producing new and unexpected results which were influential beyond the field of psychology. There was also the fact that psychology was given a greater status earlier in American universities than in the UK, and consequently America led the rest of the world in the sheer volume of research papers that were published.

Now this in itself would not really be a problem, but for the fact that American evidence of psychological investigations is accepted by many people as being generalisable on a global scale. Therefore people are assessed on the basis of these findings and judged accordingly, and it is this 'self-centredness' which is the basis of ethnocentrism. It follows that if you see yourself as the correct 'centre of the universe', other people who do not match up to or agree with you and your norms must be abnormal, unusual or in the wrong.

The idea that something which was discovered through psychological research in the US should be the same everywhere is a totally naïve view. I have to admit that when I recently visited the US for the first time, I felt that I really was in a different country, even though we both speak the same language. In fact, even though I visited only a small area (Washington and Virginia), I found the differences between our two cultures quite phenomenal. The other thing worth mentioning is that the US is a vast country consisting of 50 different states that are like countries in their own right, with their own laws and customs and traditions, so that even generalising from one side of America to the other may give rise to problems. If research comes from the US, I suppose we really ought to take into account where it was conducted because this might influence the generalisability of the findings. After all, the modern lifestyles of the inhabitants of New York in the east are totally different from those of people living in Arizona in the western part of the USA, where the pace is far slower and life more traditional.

What we have to remember is that even though we may try not to be, all of us are ethnocentric to a certain extent. That is, we judge others according to our own standards and experiences. If they are different, we are tempted to suggest that they are actually inferior to us, because we do not want to make ourselves feel inferior to them. As a result, we are clearly not being as objective as we should be. Although ethnocentrism is regarded as a weakness in psychological research, it is understandable. If you remember work by psychologists such as Sherif (1956) and Tajfel (1970), you

Figure 7.1 This rural town in Alaska is a far cry from the streets of New York City

will be aware of the fact that humans do have in-group preferences and discriminate against the out-group.

Sherif set up a situation at a boy's summer camp where ethnocentrism could flourish. He demonstrated that by making the two groups of boys aware of each other, and letting them think that they were being treated unequally, they became extremely hostile towards each other. It took a number of measures to try to diffuse the feelings between the groups. They had become positively prejudiced towards their own group and negatively prejudiced or overtly hostile towards the other.

The research by Tajfel (1970) succeeded in showing that randomly assigning people to groups was enough to make them demonstrate in-group preferences and out-group discrimination.

It has been suggested that the reason why we favour our own group is to make us feel good about ourselves. After all, we would not want to be a member of a group that we believe is inferior. We therefore 'inflate' the importance or evaluation of our own group in order to achieve this.

Most researchers are aware of the concept of ethnocentricity, but being aware of it does not always reduce it. I can try to illustrate this concept in terms of **education** with a hypothetical example using two stereotypical images. If a certain teacher has a belief that black students from other cultures are less academically able than white British students, that teacher may well treat them accordingly. What the teacher may not be aware of is that these students have a number of abilities which are not considered relevant to the assessment of educational success in the UK, for example football or music. The teacher is therefore being ethnocentric by not actually looking at the whole spectrum of student abilities – they are just looking at specific areas. This kind of ethnocentrism, where some students are perceived to be more able than others according to a limited set of criteria, can result in a kind of 'self-fulfilling prophecy' i.e. where people end up doing what is expected of them.

> Brophy and Good (1970) discovered that children who achieved higher marks (according to the school's criteria) were praised more than low-achieving pupils. This may have made the high-achieving pupils feel better about themselves, and perhaps motivated them to work even harder.

As a teacher, it is essential that all students' work is marked objectively, but it is extremely hard to judge people that you know well in a totally objective way. Because you know the students well, you are more likely to perceive their work in a more favourable light. This is why people who teach GCSEs and A levels are not allowed to mark the work of their own students. Although they are professionals who know that there is a mark scheme to abide by, they may still be somewhat subjective and not be able to look at their own students' work dispassionately.

When researchers become aware that by using European or American participants their findings will be limited in terms of universal generalisability, they may try to improve their research by broadening the types of participants who take part. Imagine that a piece of research has been designed carefully and the results analysed according to a checklist of expected results. The researchers believe that they have found out something significant which will have a large impact on the world. However, the method used may have originally been designed for white, western, middle-class men, and did not take into account the variation in possible answers due to the inclusion of the new participants.

As children mature, they demonstrate different levels of ability. Educational psychologists attempt to quantify changes in children's ability by using some kind of measurement. An example of a measuring tool can be taken from work done on children's drawings. As children get older, they demonstrate their knowledge of the world through the features they include in their drawings. A useful measuring tool of children's ability is therefore a checklist of features we would expect to see included by children at certain ages. Also we could include a score for realism, that is, where the child draws what it sees, not what it knows.

Alyson Davis (1983) looked at realism in four- and five-year-old children and included in her checklist of expected features a score for realism, whereby children draw what they know rather than what they see.

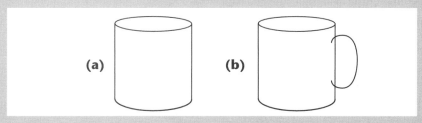

(a)   **(b)**

Figure 7.2

The children were shown cups with the handle turned away (a). Most of the children drew the handle on the mug (b), even though they couldn't see it, because they wanted the researcher to know that they knew that cups have handles. Only the children who drew (a) got a score for realism.

This measuring tool does not cause a problem for westernised children because the drawing (a) is ultimately what they would produce as they get older and realise that they do not have to demonstrate all the features of an object in their drawings – western art styles do not have this requirement. The problem occurs if we decide to use the same tool to assess the development of children from different cultures.

We would already have an idea of the standard score that children of different ages would achieve in the realism drawing test. Standardised scores are calculated by taking a group of scores from the population under investigation (in this case children) and calculating the mean (average) score. This is supposed to be representative of the 'average child' from that population and other children can therefore be assessed according to that average. If the standardised scores were calculated from a group of white, western children they would be very different from a selection of children from, say, the Tsimshian Indians of British Columbia, who draw split-style drawings which show all the important parts of the object as if it had been folded out flat.

Since this is the kind of style that the Tsimshian children would aspire to, they are unlikely to score high on the realism scale and therefore appear to be way behind western children in terms of ability (although western children would actually find the Tsimshian Indian style of drawing quite difficult) – a classic example of ethnocentrism.

Figure 7.3 *The stylised bear of the Tsimshian Indians*
By Ilil Arbel, from 'Pictorial perception and culture', by Jan B. Deregowski, © 1972 by Scientific American Inc. All rights reserved.

Further examples of ethnocentrism in measuring tools can be found in the field of **occupational psychology**. Many organisations employ occupational psychologists to recruit new personnel. The idea is that occupational psychologists will use valid selection methods to check out the suitability of applicants, and this will result in the hiring of the right person for the job. The problem here is that these selection methods are not always appropriate. Take for example the occupational personality questionnaire (OPQ) which is a psychometric test used in industry to try and assess the nature of the individual applying for a specific job. The OPQ asks people to make what are known as forced choices. This means that they have to choose, from a number of different statements, the one that describes them best, and the one that is least like them. Below is an extreme example of how difficult it can be to decide in forced choice questions.

> **Choose the statement which is most like you and enter it in box 1. Then choose the statement which is least like you and enter it in box 2.**
> - I sometimes get upset when people criticise me.
> - Criticism can be an aid to self-improvement.
> - When people criticise I ignore their comments.
> - I have confidence in myself.
>
> Box 1 ☐   Box 2 ☐

This is easier if the person concerned is literate and has a good sound knowledge of the nuances of the English language, but sometimes it is extremely hard to make forced choices when many of the statements asked do not apply to you.

If we make the comparison between some of the selection methods used by psychologists today, and the use of IQ tests as described by Gould (1982), it highlights how we must be aware of the problems that can arise using inappropriate tests. Gould looked at the consequences of judging people from other cultures by IQ tests which had been designed in North America. This was a classic demonstration of how ethnocentrism can result in the labelling of people from different cultures as being less intelligent.

In contrast, environmental studies that have looked at territoriality have investigated by observation the differences in the use of territorial markers, such as towels, bags, radios, beach toys and other paraphernalia, to mark out people's claim to space on a beach. The standard distances have been compared between cultures rather than simply judging them in comparison with western cultures. These studies lack ethnocentricity because they do not require people to become involved in designated activities and the results are not judged against a 'norm' but are simply looked at in terms of cross-cultural comparisons.

Figure 7.4 *Territorial markers on the beach*

I am sure you are now aware that most research is prone to a degree of ethnocentrism. In fact, you could evaluate any research as being ethnocentric unless it has been undertaken by a group of multi-cultural psychologists using participants from all over the world. In defence of most of the research done, it is important to remember that research funding is usually only available for limited groups of people and so the researchers themselves are not always to blame for the biased nature of their findings. It is only when they fail to take into account the limitations of their research and use it to judge others that we can truly criticise.

The key concepts of ethnocentrism
- Judging other people by our own values even though those values may not be appropriate.
- Seeing people as inferior in comparison with ourselves.

In order to evaluate research in terms of ethnocentrism, apply the following questions to the study:

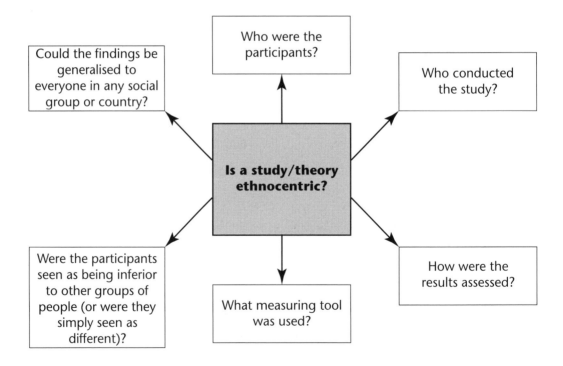

Figure 7.5

CULTURAL RELATIVISM •

From our discussion on ethnocentrism, it should be fairly obvious that different cultures have different values and beliefs and consequently their behaviour can be evaluated only in terms of their own culture. It's very unlikely that many of the findings from American research are applicable to the UK, let alone other countries. If you imagine the diversity of lifestyles, family patterns, religious beliefs, skills and abilities that each culture possesses, not to mention differences in the food they eat, the goods they produce and the environments they grow up in, it makes you realise that the likelihood of finding two similar cultural groups across the globe is very remote.

The term 'cultural relativism' (sometimes referred to as 'cultural relativity') refers to the fact that certain behaviours are relative to the culture of that person and these behaviours will have been learned. If we wish to evaluate studies which look at the behaviours of people from different cultures, we must be aware that the findings of such research must be explained in terms of how relative it is to *that* culture.

Sometimes researchers who don't take into account cultural relativism can be said to be ethnocentric. Just to clarify the difference between the two concepts: ethnocentrism is the judging of others by our own values; cultural relativism is where other people's behaviour (which is not being judged according to our values) is explained by the nature of the culture in which they have been brought up.

If we take a country which has a **collectivist** culture, we would find that the attitudes of its people differ enormously from our own culture which is an **individualist** culture. In a collectivist culture, the members believe the interests of the group as a whole are more important than those of the individual, and as such will direct their behaviour to benefitting the group rather than fulfilling their own desires. In some respects it is almost an idealised form of socialism. The members of a collectivist culture are socialised into accepting this shared responsibility for and awareness of the group, and their moral responsibilities are shaped accordingly. In an individualist culture it is the individual who is the most important element and as such the members will go about trying to satisfy their own wants and needs with little concern for the whole. 'Margaret Thatcher's England' emphasised capitalism and individual achievement as traits which were worth pursuing – the total opposite of socialism.

This idea that each person is only a part of the whole and the collective good is more important than that of the individual, is very different from the values of our society which focuses more on the individual and his or her own achievements.

One example of a collectivist culture is given by Mbiti (1970) who described how in African philosophical tradition, the individual is only part of the 'collective self' and is therefore really almost valueless. He explains that in certain African tribes counting people was forbidden because they were no more than a small part of 'society' and society was the observable whole.

Figure 7.6 *Margaret Thatcher as Prime Minister*
© AP Photo/Dennis Redman

Interestingly, this idea of collectivist cultures versus individualistic cultures seems to reflect the economic situation of the country. Collectivist cultures tend to have scarce resources and it is essential that all members of the community pull their weight in order to provide food and shelter for its members, e.g. the primitive agricultural communities. The **hunter–gatherer societies** that do not need to grow food are the richer societies. They acquire what they need by other means such as force or barter, and they have much more freedom to seek out goods and services without being tied in one place to the land. They are therefore more likely to encourage members to become more assertive, in order to gather greater amounts. Consequently, the more successful members of the community will have a higher standard of living overall as they need to depend only on themselves.

Many Japanese bring up their children to value close family relationships and the family is of prime importance to them. Mothers are very attentive to their children, spending most of their time with them and rarely leaving them with others. They encourage the children to develop within this group identity and if there are problems, the solutions are looked for by the group rather than the individual. You can see how this might explain why Japan as a nation is very successful economically – the workers work together for the common good. This ideology is totally different from the way of life adopted by many Americans (who also achieve a high level of economic success). However, Japanese people often frown upon the American way of life, finding it hard to understand why American children are encouraged to be independent and assertive and are less willing to negotiate in order to achieve harmony.

An example of how important cultural relativism is to understanding the way a society functions is to look at leadership, within both **organisational** and **sports psychology**. In western cultures, a group must have some kind of leader, be they a task-oriented leader who is most concerned with getting the job done, or a socio-emotional leader who is concerned with the welfare of the members of the group. Fiedler's Contingency Model (1967) actually suggests that the degree of power a leader has over a situation is dependent on how their style suits that situation; for example, task-oriented leaders may produce better results in times of crisis. If we decided to investigate leadership in other cultures, we would have to take into account the fact that the dominant religion of that culture or the familial patterns may result in there being no overall leader.

Imagine a group of researchers (who are unaware of specific cultural differences) decides that it wants to give new research into leadership a more universal relevance than research done in the past. They rush off to unexplored tropical islands and ask the leaders from primitive tribes questions about least preferred co-workers. First of all (if there was no language barrier), the native leaders would probably have absolutely no idea what they were talking about. The researchers may try to explain, saying that they wondered who was the person the leaders disliked most amongst the people they ruled and who was the person they found most difficult to work with! Fiedler's Contingency Model of leadership uses just this method, called the 'least preferred co-worker scale', when investigating leadership styles. Supposing they didn't have a culture where one person was in a position of power over another in the same way that we do within our workplace. Even if they did manage to identify someone, they would then have to try and work out what the next task was – potential language difficulties? What the researchers should have done is realise that cultural relativism makes some tasks inappropriate for some cultures; their culture should have been considered for its own worth.

In **health psychology**, researchers have been interested in looking at the instances of **anorexia nervosa** amongst the population, trying to understand the phenomenon whereby people may actually starve themselves to death. Many researchers claim that the media are responsible for the prevalence of anorexia, due to the promotion of the slim (if not skinny) ideal body shape for women. However, it is worth remembering that anorexia actually predates modern media images although it has become much more prevalent in the western world in the last forty years, during which time models have gone from the curvaceous figures of people like Marilyn Monroe and Jane Mansfield to women like Kate Moss, who some might argue looks almost pre-pubescent.

Although anorexia is now sometimes found in developing countries, the causes of anorexia would be incomprehensible to someone from a third-world country who has serious food shortages.

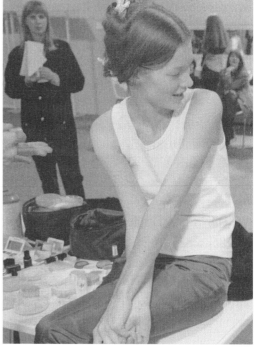

Figure 7.7 *Marilyn Monroe and Kate Moss epitomise two totally different body shapes, reflecting the fashions of the time*

Criminal psychologists investigating marital violence, have discovered that in some cultures marital violence is more acceptable than in others. Smith (1990) suggests that marital violence is associated with societies that are strongly patriarchal. These societies see males as the legitimately dominant partners in marriage and are therefore more likely to accept instances of domestic violence by the husband towards his wife. Other research has indicated that patriarchal societies tend to have a long history of warfare, and therefore the men and women have different roles within that society. The men are the warriors and the women are the child-bearers and home-makers. The boys are taken from their mothers and initiated into the role of 'male dominance' and therefore lose any of the more feminine traits, because to demonstrate any sort of 'feminine weakness' would be seen as humiliating.

Research into family violence must take into account that this situation occurs and use it as a basis on which to understand different patterns of behaviour. If these cultural differences are not considered, the behaviour of some of the participants will be seen as socially unacceptable according to western standards, where wife-beating is generally condemned. If the behaviour is regarded within a cultural context, it does not make the behaviour any more acceptable but it makes it more understandable. Understanding the causes of behaviours make them easier to deal with. We must also remember that any judgement that forgets cultural differences is really ethnocentric.

Cultural relativity and ethics

Finally, it is essential to consider the methodology used when investigating a specific concept using multi-cultural participants. Consider the differences in male and female roles in different societies and imagine that we asked members of one culture to do something which goes against religious beliefs or values. Two general examples spring to mind here – testing the effects of alcohol on Muslim participants, and also asking strict Muslim women and men to rate each other for facial attractiveness when the women usually wear Yashmaks (the double veils worn by Muslim women in public which leave only their eyes visible). Such research would be totally unethical, as it could subject the participants to high levels of anxiety.

> **The central features of cultural relativity are:**
> *   Being aware of the different aspects of the cultures under investigation when planning research.
> *   Making the methodology appropriate for the culture under investigation.
> *   Ensuring that cultural diversity is taken into account when interpreting research findings.

In order to evaluate whether research has taken into account cultural relativity, apply the questions on the next page to the study.

ECOLOGICAL VALIDITY

One of the most frequent misconceptions is that research which is conducted in a laboratory lacks what we commonly call **ecological validity**. In fact, the term 'ecological validity' refers to the extent to which results can be generalised beyond the present setting, so although you may conduct research in a laboratory, it doesn't automatically mean that it is not valid in other environments. Similarly, you may carry out some sort of research in a naturalistic environment, but it may just as well lack ecological validity because the results are only valid in the setting you have chosen.

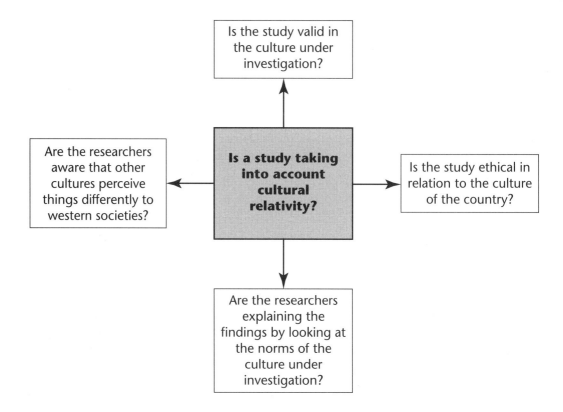

Figure 7.8

In order to explain clearly the idea of ecological validity rather than using it in its simplest, and often mistaken context, I will have to explain some of the related terms. In fact, the concept of ecological validity really dates back to Egon Brunswik who was involved in investigating visual perception during the 1950s. He was particularly interested in the effects of visual cues as an aid to perception and the difference between the cues available within and outside the laboratory. However, the more general use of the term within the area of research methods can be attributed to Campbell and Stanley (1966), who established its meaning in the context of external validity as compared with internal validity.

1 **Internal validity** really refers to whether the study is actually valid at all, i.e. whether the study really did show the effects of the independent variable on the dependent variable (if the study didn't have internal validity – it means that the results were caused by some other confounding variable).

2 **External validity** refers to whether the findings can be generalised beyond the present study to hold true for other groups of people in different locations, at different times and using different methodologies to measure the same concept.

The idea of external validity can be broken down still further into:

- **population validity** – the extent to which results could be generalised to other populations of people.
- **ecological validity** – the extent to which results can be generalised beyond the present setting.

What we have to be aware of is that studies which are conducted in the 'real world' (naturalistic setting) may also lack ecological validity. In order to find out whether a study really does have ecological validity we must actually test out the result in other settings, and if the results are the same, then, and only then, can we be sure.

It is often suggested that Milgram's (1963) original study into obedience lacked ecological value. In this study, he discovered that 65 per cent of the participants were willing to give a complete stranger fatal electric shocks, but again we would not know this unless the findings were tested elsewhere. Milgram then conducted a number of follow-up studies, which were taken out of Yale university and into a downtown office block. He still found extraordinary levels of obedience on the part of his participants, although they were now in a totally different environment. This gave support to his conclusions; it also removed some of the criticisms that the original study lacked ecological validity because it was carried out within a university. In contrast, Hofling *et al.*'s (1966) study of obedience among nurses in a hospital was conducted in a naturalistic setting.

Hofling's study involved nurses being asked to administer double the maximum daily dose of a drug to a patient, on the telephone orders of a doctor. The findings were that 21 out of 22 nurses obeyed the telephone orders.

However, if we believe that naturalistic settings automatically qualify for 'ecological validity' and therefore result in more valid findings, in this instance we would be wrong. Replications of the study have failed to produce the same results, so these results were confined to this specific 'natural' setting at this specific time.

Therefore, when evaluating research, we must always question whether we think a study has ecological validity, even though we can never be absolutely sure. It is not hard to imagine how many of the studies carried out in laboratories lacked ecological validity; after all, simply bringing subjects into a new environment where they are asked to do something contrived by someone else will have an effect on their behaviour. Much of the research carried out on children, such as the study conducted by Bandura (1961) in which small children were shown how to beat up a large inflatable doll by an adult, must lack ecological validity. How many times in the real world do we see adults beating up a large inflatable doll? Yet the findings from this study have been cited in many areas of psychology such as **criminal psychology** and **sports psychology** as an explanation of how we learn violent behaviours.

Another very familiar example which is often cited within many areas of psychology is the work of Elizabeth Loftus, who suggested that eyewitness memory is influenced by a number of factors besides the situation itself.

In one study, Loftus and Palmer (1974) showed their participants videos of car accidents and suggested that their findings related to real-life eyewitness testimony. In another study Loftus *et al.* (1987) showed participants a film of a customer holding either a gun or a cheque book in a restaurant and concluded that participants found it easier to identify the person holding the cheque than the gun, because in the gun condition they focused more on the gun than the person.

Figure 7.9 *How much will he accurately remember?*

Although the findings of Loftus make sense, it must be remembered that the research lacks ecological validity. After all, we would respond very differently in a real-life situation to someone brandishing a gun in a restaurant or a car accident happening before our very eyes.

In the area of **health psychology**, questionnaires are regularly used to measure levels of pain and stress. One of the most famous questionnaires used to gain information about pain is the McGill Pain Questionnaire (Melzack, 1975). This questionnaire asks participants to ring words that best describe their pain from a list of 78 possible pain descriptions. The words are grouped together in different categories, which cover sensory, emotional and evaluative aspects of pain feelings and participants are asked to ring one word from each category. An example of some of the words used are 'flickering, tearing, cruel, lancinating and dreadful', all of which, if they are understood, will mean different things to different people. How can a list of words truly give an idea of the experience of pain? In this case, the methods used may well lack ecological validity, because sitting in a room, filling in a questionnaire is perhaps not really a valid measurement of how a person really feels about the situation in their everyday life. In order to make sure that the measurement has any kind of ecological validity we would have to try and find an alternative way of measuring pain on a day to day basis whilst the participant is continuing their everyday life, and this in itself is a problem. Even observation of someone's behaviour does not actually give you an idea of the amount of pain they are experiencing, and this is the problem with research into pain.

Another example of the difference between real-life situations and psychological studies comes from the work conducted in 1945 by Mackworth, who was interested in looking at the topic of attention (Mackworth, 1950). Paying attention is essential in some areas of sports and so **sports psychologists** have considered past research in order to understand the topic. Research into attention began after the Second World War when there was considerable interest in the ability to pay attention to specific stimuli for prolonged periods of time. The focus of interest was radar operators who were looking for enemy aircraft or submarines and the question being asked was how long they could sustain their attention without losing concentration. This topic is of interest to all of us today too, with the skies becoming more and more busy with an ever-increasing number of aircraft flying all over the globe.

> Mackworth gave his participants a laboratory task where they had to watch a clock on which the second hand moved one step every second for two hours. Twelve times every 30 minutes, at random, the pointer would jump two steps and the participants had to respond by pressing a key. The results indicated that performance was 85 per cent correct in the first 30 minutes, but then progressively declined. It was discovered that feedback increased the likelihood of performance remaining high but the level of arousal of subjects also contributed to performance, with subjects who had frequent signals remaining more alert than others.

I am surprised that any of his participants were actually awake at the end of the two hours. The difference between such a study and a real-life situation, where people's lives are at risk, does not need explaining. The lack of ecological validity here speaks for itself. The trouble again is that we could not risk putting lives in jeopardy in the name of research. Of course there are alternative ways of doing the studies, such as convincing the participants that they really were in charge of people's lives whilst showing them pre-recorded radar pictures, but here we come back to the question of ethics.

In contrast to some of the studies above, there are some studies which do seem to have ecological validity; these are field experiments where participants are observed in everyday situations and their behaviour is looked at in context and interpreted accordingly. As we mentioned earlier, the investigation of territorial behaviour in **environmental psychology** has involved looking at the use of territorial markers in refectories and playgrounds – in these cases the participants are observed in a natura-listic environment with no awareness that people are watching them, so their behaviour should be unaffected. In **educational psychology**, the investigation and testing of children within classrooms will have a high level of ecological validity as the children will be used to having their abilities measured in a classroom situation and are unlikely to find any further testing unusual.

Perhaps some of the most amazing studies which actually have a large measure of ecological validity come from the area of **environmental psychology**.

> Poulton *et al.* (1975) were interested in looking at the effects of the wind on partic-ipant's behaviours. They exposed female participants to winds of between 9 and 20 mph, which varied in degrees of turbulence; these winds were not natural winds, however. They were actually created in a wind tunnel and were supposed to mimic winds which were strong enough to be noticeable and cause slight discomfort, or winds which were very uncomfortable and would inhibit performance. The partici-pants were asked to do a number of tasks with the expectation that the wind would inhibit performance. The results were that wind did in fact cause the participants problems in the tasks that were set.

When I first read about Poulton's work, my first thoughts were that anyone put in a wind tunnel would have a fairly reasonable expectation as to what was likely to hap-pen, therefore the research actually has a high level of ecological validity in terms of performance (although the studies may have been lacking in terms of autonomic arousal). I don't know if you have ever seen a film of anyone in a wind tunnel, leaning against the blasting air. It looks to me like it might be quite good fun, and I am sure I would get the giggles. Not quite the same as being in the real wind, which can actually be a bit frightening because at least you would know that the person in charge of the controls could switch off the wind if the results became too extreme. There were advan-tages of having the study in the wind tunnel, and that is the control of extraneous variables such as air temperature and humidity. However, the tasks that the subjects were required to do are themselves somewhat bizarre. They were asked to walk in a straight line, pour water into a wine glass, put on a raincoat and tie a headscarf (how many people nowadays wear headscarves besides the Queen?). The number of times they blinked in a certain period was also counted and they were timed picking selected words from a list and finding a circled word in a newspaper. Why? Would we really do this in a strong wind?

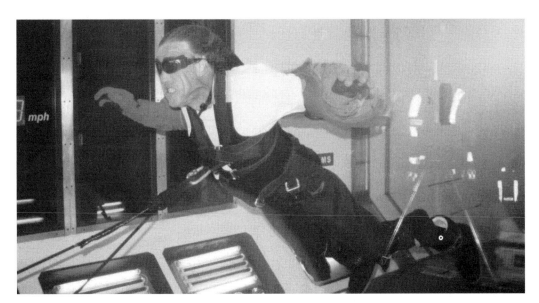

Figure 7.10 *Jeremy Clarkson, with a bit more wind in his hair than usual, in the BBC series* Speed
© *BBC Picture Archives*

I have to be honest and say that when I first read about these studies, I found them really amusing. My first thoughts were that they seemed to lack any sort of ecological validity – but when I thought about it, they are actually very well designed. Yes, I accept that the levels of arousal would be different, but how else could the studies have been conducted? Wind does not blow according to researchers' needs and humidity and air temperature do vary. If there is a fairly strong wind and the air temperature is hot, the wind is a welcome relief. If, on the other hand, the air temperature is cold, the wind makes it worse and the perception of the wind would be much more negative. Therefore the studies must be judged bearing both these points in mind. It makes the lack of ecological validity seem less ridiculous, but it also means that we should not take the findings as an indication of everyone's likely response in all situations.

Mathews and Canon (1975) were interested in the effects of noise on pro-social (helping) behaviour and they set up a laboratory experiment and also a field experiment to investigate how noise may influence people.

> Their naïve subjects had been asked to attend a laboratory to take part in an exper-
> iment. Whilst they were waiting for the experiment to start, they were asked to wait
> in the lab with a confederate of the researcher who was sitting down, reading a
> journal with a number of other books and journals on their lap. Whilst they were
> waiting, the subjects were exposed to one of a number of different levels of noise
> through a hidden speaker. After a short time, the experimenter called the confeder-
> ate who stood up, dropping the items that had been on their lap on the floor in
> front of the subject.

The point of the experiment was to measure whether or not the subject helped the
confederate and it was found that, the louder the noise, the less likely the subject was
to help.

This experiment, although carried out in a laboratory, has a reasonable level of
ecological validity because the participant was expecting to be there anyway and the
situation that occurred was reasonably true to life. If the participants were students,
which seems quite likely, they would also have been relatively familiar with the environment, giving the study more ecological validity.

It's strange how most psychology students don't recognise the fact that sometimes
a laboratory can be a familiar environment to research participants – so it is worth
trying to find out who the participants were. After all, if they went into one of the
labs at college where they usually had lessons, then they would be on familiar territory. If you are unable to get that level of information, then simply be aware (and
state in your work) that if they were students, they probably wouldn't have found the
environment as threatening perhaps as other members of the public.

The researchers exposed the subjects to either 48 dB of normal noise (what is normal?), 65 dB of white noise (which contains many frequencies all of equal intensity)
or 85 dB of white noise. I wonder if the participants thought the blasts of noise were
unusual. Perhaps this factor may have somewhat reduced the ecological validity,
because one would be unlikely to hear white noise at that level in an everyday setting. This in turn may have given the participants some inkling that something was
going on! We are also not told whether participants had their hearing tested prior to
the study. I would not suggest using this as a major evaluative issue, as differences in
hearing acuity are probably not great amongst the population. It would be better to
mention simply the individual differences between participants in their response to
noise which may have affected their perception of the noise.

The confederate may have indicated some kind of 'experimenter effect' on the subject by imposing an expectation of the way in which they should behave. You might
conjecture that the participant also had some idea of what the study was about by
having talked to friends. They may also have felt that they did not want to look

unhelpful to the researcher, whom they would be seeing alone very soon. After all, we all want people to think the best of us. However, as studies go, this one is fairly well thought-out and unlikely to suffer from too many methodological weaknesses.

The second part of the experiment involved a confederate dropping a box of books while getting out of a car. In half the trials, he wore a plaster cast on his arm and in half the trials he was fine. Noise was varied by having another confederate with a lawnmower nearby. In half the trials, the lawnmower was running (87 dB) and in the other half, it was silent. However, the background noise was still quite loud, measuring 50 dBs.

The researchers observed helping behaviour and found that noise had little effect on helping behaviour when the subject didn't have a plaster cast on. (There was little difference between the lawnmower and no lawnmower condition, participants showing 10 per cent and 20 per cent helping behaviour respectively.) On the other hand, when the confederate was wearing the plaster cast, people helped 80 per cent of the time when the lawnmower was silent, but only 15 per cent of the time when it was running.

Again, the conclusion from this study is that noise does influence our likelihood of helping.

Do you feel that the second study is more ecologically valid than the first or do they both score highly on the ecological validity scale? The second study involved participants who were simply members of the public, going about their business in a naturalistic environment with a lawnmower running which would be a normal sight in the summer months (provided there is grass for them to mow). Therefore it would seem likely that the second study was also ecologically valid.

Within all areas of psychology there are numerous examples of studies which lack ecological validity, from the original laboratory experiments to the more recent applied areas undertaken in naturalistic environments. As long as we are aware of the weaknesses of these designs, the research still maintains some validity – validity in the environment where it was undertaken.

The central features which ensure that research has ecological validity are:
- The researchers have seriously considered where the study should be undertaken and have decided that the location is appropriate. (The artificiality of laboratory set-ups is often required for certain studies and is an excellent way to isolate variables and provide powerful, unbiased evidence for theory.)

> • The results of the study are generalisable to any sort of environment, irrespective of where it has been undertaken.
> • If the study is conducted in a laboratory or 'unnatural' environment, it must have been designed well enough to ensure that the findings of the study can be related to real life and not just to laboratory research, and similarly, that if it is conducted in a naturalistic environment, it is not simply related to that environment alone, but could be found elsewhere.

In order to evaluate whether research is ecologically valid, apply the following questions to the study:

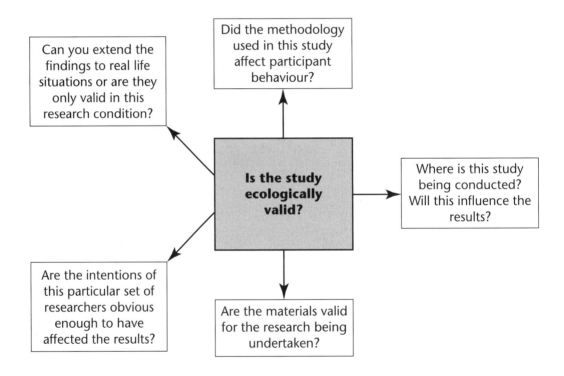

Figure 7.11

IS THE RESEARCH RECENT? • • • • • • • • • • • • • • • • • •

When I was little, televisions were relatively rare and I remember getting our first black and white television and being so excited. I actually believed there were little people in the television set, like a Punch and Judy show, and they were acting for me.

I often wonder whether television had much of an influence on my behaviour, bearing in mind that the programmes were initially quite primitive ('Bill and Ben the Flowerpot Men' and 'The Woodentops' – all of whom were obviously puppets). If you compare them with children's television today, where programmes such as Power Rangers and Grange Hill have a much higher degree of realism, I would imagine that the influence they have on children would be considerably different. The question is, *how* different? Would they have more or less influence on children? Perhaps I was more likely to be influenced by television as it was so novel and new, whereas children today are more critical and demand more and more sophistication from their programmes. On the other hand, the simple fact that today's programmes are realistic may make them more influential. These suggestions indicate that research such as Bandura's Bobo doll research may not produce the same results as in 1961.

Taking this argument one stage further, think of the kind of role models which are available for children today. If we accept the findings of Bandura – that children copy role models and are more likely to imitate those who are of the same gender and more powerful, this could explain why there is more female violence today. **Criminal psychologists** have investigated the type of models available in arcade games. In 1985, Toles found from a sample of 100 video arcade games that 92 per cent did not include any female roles. Today the situation is very different. Lara Croft is one of the most familiar arcade heroines, and in all the fighting games there are always female combatants who are as capable as any man of decimating their rivals with their numerous skills.

Many of the key studies which have shaped our understanding of human behaviour and cognition are dated and may possibly produce different results if undertaken today. The Milgram (1963) study of obedience would, I believe, produce very different results today, where people are taught from an early age to challenge and question rather than blindly accept facts. Today's psychology students come from that background and are taught, as part of their psychology courses, to evaluate and question the findings of research – very different to the psychology undergraduates of yesteryear who accepted the information given with less scepticism. If we recall that much of the research of the past used those particular psychology students as subjects, it would make sense that today's findings would be considerably different.

We must not forget that laws change and this influences the behaviour of different groups in society, especially the participants in research undertaken by criminal psychologists. The law which made homosexuality a criminal offence no longer exists and there is a growing lobby attempting to change the age of consent for homosexuals to 16. In the past, participants in psychological research may have given socially acceptable answers rather than admit they were breaking the law. Research into marital rape has also been affected by changes in the law. Until the late

1970s the law did not recognise marital rape, believing that it was a man's right to have sexual intercourse with his wife. Imagine the results of research prior to that date which considered aggression within marriage.

Other factors might influence the participant responses gained today by some groups within society. Ethnic groups are more widely integrated and accepted in many walks of life, whereas in the 1960s there was still considerable suspicion about different cultures. Today women are now more able to fulfil their potential, both educationally and in career choices. In fact women today have far greater status in the workplace than they did in the 1950s and 1960s; much of the early research into organisations excluded women from the samples and those that were included would probably have had far less confidence and status than the women of the twenty-first century. In fact within organisational psychology, early studies of women that were carried out indicated that they lacked self-confidence and were frightened of success, having been socialised into fulfilling no more than the 'little wife at home' image. Any women who did achieve success were perceived as possessing masculine traits as these were believed to be essential prerequisites to success. Today's research would produce a very different picture, although highly successful women are still in the minority. However, the women who achieve success are often valued more objectively for the individuality they bring to management roles, and the idea that they are always people-orientated is no longer a universal perception.

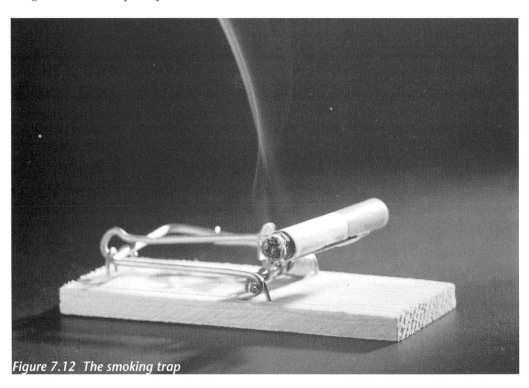

Figure 7.12 The smoking trap

In health psychology, addiction to cigarette smoking has provided the basis for considerable amounts of research for a long period of time. In the 1930s and 1940s cigarettes were not believed to be harmful and cigarette smoking was the norm. Instances of death from lung cancer in America were about 5 per 100,000 in contrast to death from breast and stomach cancer, which were about five times as high. The incidence of lung cancer began to rise between 15 and 20 years after smoking rates rose, and matched the rise in cigarette use, although men were the most prevalent users of cigarettes. At the time of writing, rates of smoking are actually higher for younger women than young men and the dangers of passive smoking have been acknowledged. In fact the whole attitude to smoking has changed enormously since the 1930s and therefore research carried out today into smoking will reflect these changes in attitude and may also affect the way the results are interpreted.

In contrast, there are a number of studies which are now dated but which would possibly provide the same results today. One of the most famous studies that fits into this category and is regularly referred to in many areas of psychology (especially within educational psychology) is the study by Rosenthal and Jacobson in 1968.

> Children were randomly selected and identified to their class teachers as being incredibly bright and having the potential to progress academically at a faster rate than other children of the same ages. At the end of the following year, the children who had been singled out were tested and proved to have lived up to their teachers' mistaken perceptions.

There were some problems with the study, in that the IQ tests given to children to assess their progress were not standardised for the age range of children in the study. Consequently, efforts at replicating the study have produced mixed results, but the overall findings have influenced the behaviour of teachers and have helped to prevent the 'labelling' of children in many cases.

> **The central features which ensure that research is current**
> * The study has been carried out in the last ten years.
> * The methodology used does not include questionnaires which were written decades prior to the commencement of the study (as are some personality tests).

In order to evaluate whether research is out of date, apply the following questions to the study:

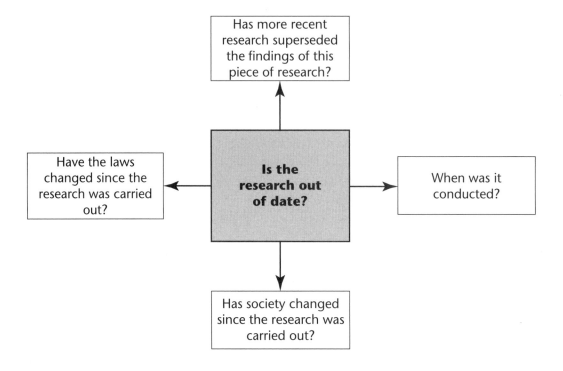

Has more recent research superseded the findings of this piece of research?

Have the laws changed since the research was carried out?

Is the research out of date?

When was it conducted?

Has society changed since the research was carried out?

Figure 7.13

SUBJECT VARIABLES ●

Most research gives a set of results which show whether the **independent variable** has affected the **dependent variable**. If these results are statistically significant, we walk away happily accepting that this or that happens in the majority of cases. There are, however, differences in the responses of participants which will affect why or how they came to behave the way that they did in the research situation, and these are to do with the individual. Let me give you an example. We can safely say that alcohol makes you drunk – an undisputed fact. However, there are a number of factors relating to the individual which will influence how drunk he or she actually becomes. These factors can be: the person's size, their metabolic rate, their familiarity with the consumption of alcohol e.g. whether or not they have a high tolerance, what they have eaten and how fast it was digested or whether something happens which suddenly has a sobering effect on them (such as parents arriving home during a party, or missing the last train). A similar situation exists within psychology. We may conclude that A generally results in B but there will be a number of factors influencing how much A affects each individual and these factors could be to do with the person's physiology or their past experiences – the things that vary between people.

In the area of **health psychology**, it has been accepted that exercise seems to reduce the negative effects of stress.

> Roth and Holmes (1985) discovered that college students who took physical exercise reported fewer stress-related health problems and depressive symptoms than other students who were less active.

The question is what were these people like? Perhaps some of the students who took exercise had higher self-esteem than others, had different personality types or had recently met a new girl- or boy-friend and felt good because of that. It may even have been the case that some of them decided to go on a low-fat, high-fibre diet and take up Yoga at the same time, whilst others went for counselling to change their perceptions. The trouble is, each one of us has a different level of tolerance for stress. We also deal with stressful situations differently and these individual differences are often overlooked when assessing the nature of psychological research.

Another set of studies, which can be compared with Roth and Holmes, come from **criminal psychology**. Studies which look at the perpetrators of child sexual abuse often brand all abusers together, without taking into account the very different nature of the abusers and the possible motives underlying the abuse. They are categorised into the stereotypical model of an abuser and yet they are often very different. Some may be no more than predatory men who are simply seeking sexual gratification, whereas others may be inadequate individuals who simply crave some sort of close physical relationship and do not perceive the relationship as being in the same category as the predators. When looking at the causes of abuse and considering treatment of such offenders, the individual differences between them must be taken into account.

Within the area of **organisational psychology**, the personality traits of leaders are often considered important in order to ascertain whether they will be effective leaders or not. However, the traits of each individual will surely interact with the people they are to lead and in some cases different leaders will be more effective. Surely these situational influences will affect whether a leader is successful and their ability to be flexible will have as much influence on their success as the personality traits they possess. Therefore the situation will influence the success or failure of a leader and the individual differences between them will explain why one person can be a successful leader but another person, put in the same situation, will be ineffective.

In order to evaluate whether research takes into account the individuality of the participants, apply the questions on the next page to the study:

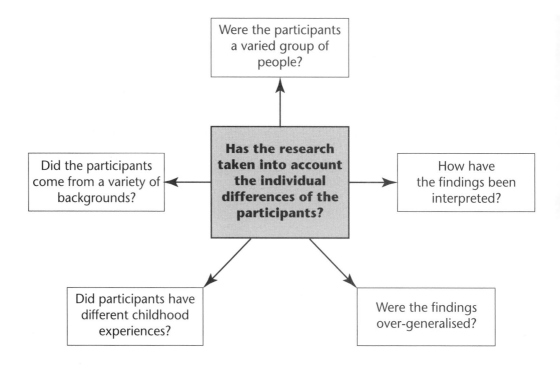

Figure 7.14

Is psychological research really useful?

8

- **Does old equal 'out of date'?**
- **Can we apply the research to new situations?**
- **What are the implications of psychological research?**

I must admit, when I read about different types of psychological research, my initial response is often totally subjective and completely ignores the weaknesses in the design. In fact this is where the tabloid newspapers often score – they choose a finding, totally out of context, and spread it all over the papers. I remember reading something in the tabloid press about levels of homosexuality. My first response was something like 'Wow, does one in five men really have gay tendencies?'. The impact of the research overwhelmed me, and I forgot to look at it evaluatively. OK, so the research on the prevalence of homosexuality was conducted in Brighton, a well-known centre for the gay community, but the initial impact was still the same. We all probably respond in a similar way and the people who are really to blame are the media. On the other hand, if you were a journalist and discovered a piece of research which looked as if it had the likelihood of selling newspapers, you too would probably use it as a topical headline and blaze it all over the papers as if it were an undisputable fact. The trouble is, we can get used to reading sensational headlines and accepting them, and yet if any of you have ever been the subject of media coverage, you probably found that the article had some kind of mistake in it.

Figure 8.1 *Would the papers record this accurately?*
© AP Photo/Mike Fisher

The first time I read about myself in a local newspaper (not that there has been much other media coverage), I was about nine years old and was the May Queen of the village I lived in at the time. It was a very small village and the May Festival was the annual event. I think I became May Queen because no one else wanted to be pulled along in a cart by the young boys of the village, especially as the cart was used for ferrying compost about! When the newspaper was put on sale, I rushed along to read about my moment of glory. On opening the page I was shocked – the person reported to be May Queen was my maid of honour, the date of the festival was wrong and what made it worse, my name was spelt incorrectly. I think it was this moment that made me more aware of the ease with which we can be misrepresented.

Looking back on it now, it seems so irrelevant and yet at the time, it felt like the end of the world. Perhaps all research reports are like this; at the time they seem to have such a huge amount of importance and yet in years to come they are out of date and really obsolete. This is where I intend to start the final section of this book – to ask you to ask yourself if the findings of past research are relevant today.

IS THE RESEARCH STILL RELEVANT OR IS IT OUT OF DATE? •

In the past, I have told my students to look at the date past research has been conducted and to try and work out if the date could explain the findings and whether or not they are relevant today. The trouble is, I found that the essays they wrote suggested that anything that was more than about fifteen years old was now completely irrelevant and that these findings would be totally different if the research was replicated now.

Well – this is not always the case. In fact much of the research conducted in the past would still produce the same results. Take, for example, the research conducted by Pavlov on classical conditioning. This was done in 1927, and yet we still have reflex responses today. Similarly the study by Watson and Rayner (1920), which induced a phobia in poor little Albert, would also be replicable today.

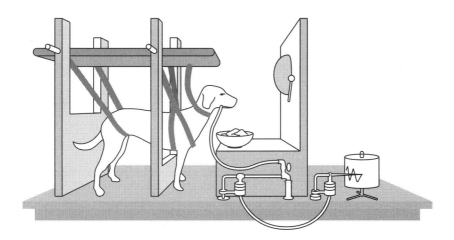

Figure 8.2 Pavlov's equipment for recording the salivation of dogs

You must take account of the research and evaluate it objectively. After all, the basic emotions that you feel are the same emotions felt by your parents and your grandparents. Let me give you an example. I am much older than the students I teach, and yet I still feel the same feelings that they feel (and if I don't, I remember what they were like when I did feel them). I still get upset and worry, I can feel inadequate, I may get angry or hostile or irritated, I still feel fear and I still know what it feels like to be in love. The fact that I started feeling these things about 30 years before my students doesn't mean the feelings themselves have changed.

Similarly with the findings of psychological research: we still need to conform, we are still obedient and we still go through the same stages of development. We also still fail to conform to health requests, feel more confident when we are at home rather than away, choose the same kinds of leaders. We continue to live up to the expectations of our teachers, are more likely to become aggressive if we have aggressive role models, and get stressed if we are in overcrowded conditions; furthermore we still attribute internal motives to others but blame our own behaviour on the situation.

You may wonder why so many things don't seem to have changed despite the advances in society. In many ways each generation thinks it knows better than the previous generation, although when you really look at the psychological research done in the past it makes you wonder! It should give you the idea that despite the sophistication of our methodologies now, people are still people and still seem to function by the same sets of rules. Perhaps behaviour is biologically programmed after all – at least that would account for the similarities in behaviours between generations in spite of such a changing environment.

Many of our responses must have some kind of biological basis – we don't like to feel uncomfortable and so the most overwhelming drive is to reduce anxiety and discomfort in whatever way we can. The thing that will most likely have changed, therefore, is our understanding of how to deal with many of these issues and that is more to do with the current values our society holds dear and our increasing knowledge of how things function.

Perhaps as a way of illustrating what I mean, let's look at these ideas in more detail. First of all consider the idea of arousal; we become aroused if we are put in a crowded situation. The nature of our physiology is such that too much stimulus leads to over-arousal and we therefore seek to reduce the arousal to a level at which we feel more comfortable. Imagine now, you are in a crowded environment, an underground train in the height of the rush hour. You are jam-packed in with hundreds of other people and you were unable to get a seat so you are hanging on to one of the poles trying not to fall over. How do you feel? Uncomfortable, hot, tense? You avert your gaze from other people, trying desperately hard not to make eye contact because if you maintain an element of 'distance' it makes it easier for you to deal with the crowding. You may actually pull out a book, or turn up your walkman as a way of

Figure 8.3 *Avoiding eye contact is a way of reducing the effects of crowding*

switching off from the overcrowded train. Now imagine that the train stops in the tunnel for a while. The crowding, along with the heat, make you more and more uptight. Someone pushes you – you snap at them irritably.

Here we have shown that arousal leads to the desire to escape (to lower the arousal level) or the potential to become aggressive. The first studies to have looked at the effects of being overcrowded on arousal were conducted as early as the 1950s. However, their findings are still relevant today although how we deal with over-crowding may be different. In the past there were few opportunities to escape to foreign locations, as the varied means of public transport was not as readily available for everyone. Nowadays, we only have to pick up a newspaper and there are adver-tisements for holidays all over the world. Simply knowing that we can escape if we need to is often sufficient to allow us to manage our high levels of arousal. After all, how many times have you told yourself that if you really don't like something, there is nothing actually *making* you continue to do it.

Now let's look at the changing values in society. Take, for example the expectation that we will live a long and healthy life rather than ageing in our sixties. Even when I was young, people in their sixties were considered old. Their expectations of life were often very different to ours and they may have been unlikely to take up new and excit-ing hobbies or challenges when they reached retirement age. The stereotypical image of the old age pensioner going and working on his allotment was often about as good as it got. Nowadays, things are very different. I know of people in their sixties who have decided to go and spend a couple of years doing voluntary service overseas, teaching in places like Africa. I have heard of people taking up flying or studying for a degree rather than hanging up their hats, putting on their slippers and waiting to die.

Figure 8.4 For some, life begins at 60

Now relate this to psychological research. Think of health psychology and the effectiveness of health promotion measures. People in middle age are now far more likely to embrace health-promoting ideas because they believe that they still have a number of years ahead of them to enjoy, and that it is better to be healthy in old age than infirm.

Another area where the changing values of society may have an impact is the nature of crime. In the past racist attitudes were not always looked upon with the contempt with which they are today. Therefore studies that have looked at stereotypical racial images may well be outdated. The idea that rape is the fault of the woman has now been turned around because certain stereotypical myths about gender relations have been exploded. Similarly, in the workplace, the expectation that women should have equal opportunities is no longer seen as bizarre (although it still may not have been totally implemented).

Finally consider the increase in our knowledge. Some people used to believe that we could be born 'evil' while others denied any genetic input into our behaviour. This was the original nature–nurture debate which we have mentioned already. Now we know that there may well be genetic predispositions to various behaviours but that they may not manifest themselves without environmental triggers. It used to be accepted that schizophrenia was caused by possession by evil spirits. We laugh at the thought nowadays, but this misunderstanding lead to the cruel treatment of schizophrenics, with the aim of making the evil spirits leave their bodies. Stoning or immersing in freezing cold water were considered suitable methods of treating people with schizophrenia. We are shocked by the barbarity of such treatments because we now *know* that many of the symptoms are due to a physiological cause – the excess of dopamine at the neuronal receptor sites.

IS THE RESEARCH USEFUL? • • • • • • • • • • • • • • • • • • •

Whether all the research we have considered actually serves any real purpose is another matter. Perhaps we are trying to find hidden meanings and causes for behaviour that is purely random! In fact, much of the research that is conducted today seems to have little or no relationship to the real world. I guess half of the reason for this is because past research has covered many of the more fundamental theories or concepts and in order for research to continue, much of it has to focus on the little nit-picking details. I randomly picked a copy of the British Journal of Psychology from my bookcase. It was dated February 2000 and contained research on such topics as 'Orienting to exogenous cues and attentional bias to affective pictures reflect separate processes' (Jason Tipples and Dinkar Sharma) and 'A new family handedness sample with findings consistent with X-linked transmission' (Walter F. McKeever). I thought to myself that such research would be unlikely to influence the world in quite the same way as Milgram or Zimbardo, and I would imagine that these pieces of research aren't particularly useful to our everyday lives. However I also looked at another piece of research in the same journal entitled 'Dogs as catalysts for social interactions: Robustness of the effect' (June McNicholas and Glyn M. Collis) and actively made the decision that even though my dog had just chewed the edge of the carpet, I would make sure that I always have one as a pet.

If you consider the research from the different areas of psychology, I am sure that you will find some more useful than others. I would like to take you back to the study taken from **environmental psychology** conducted in a wind tunnel that I talked about in Chapter 7. If you remember, Poulton *et al.* (1975) were interested in looking at the effects of the wind on participants' behaviours. The findings were (amongst others) that they had problems in pouring water from a jug, had trouble tying a headscarf and finding a circled word in a newspaper. Well – how useful have you found that information?

On the other hand, studies such as the Elizabeth Loftus studies on the fragility of memory and the inaccuracy of eyewitness testimony are extremely useful in the area of **criminal psychology**, even though they were conducted in the 1970s. The acceptance that memory is not like a tape recorder has influenced court procedures to the extent that eyewitness testimony alone is insufficient to convict a criminal. Further work by Loftus (1979) has illustrated how a previous association between two factors can be worked into the memory of later events where those factors are no longer associated. Loftus showed participants a short film of one person talking to another. Later in the film the second person is seen committing a burglary with an unseen accomplice. When participants were asked about the film, they remembered the accomplice as the person they had seen in the early part of the film purely as a result of the previous association between the two characters.

This has tremendous usefulness if we consider the terrible real-life situation that was reported by Aronson *et al.* in 1999. One hundred and sixty-eight people were killed when the federal buildings in Oklahoma City were blown up on 19th April, 1995. Tom Kessinger, who was a truck rental office mechanic said he saw Timothy McVeigh (who was later convicted) enter the office with another man to rent a van the day before the bombings. It turned out that the other man, who was briefly described by Kessinger and subsequently hunted by the police, had in fact rented a different truck the day before the bombing. Kessinger had simply unconsciously transferred one memory to the next so that he was unable to differentiate between the two. If eyewitness testimony had been accepted, the innocent man may well have been convicted.

Another example of how research has proved useful is the work of Bowlby (1953) which, although somewhat extreme, led to the encouragement of mothers to stay in hospital with their children if they had to remain as inpatients for a period of time.

Figure 8.5 *Timothy McVeigh – the Oklahoma City bomber*
© AP Photo/John Gaps III

Because young children are unable to rationalise in the same way as adults, they may well have felt deserted and this, in turn, may have lead to feelings of insecurity and despair. After all, much research (Ainsworth *et al.,* 1978) has shown that initially, children who are firmly 'attached' to their caregiver, cry and become extremely distressed when left. They then seem to go through a period of depression and finally become relatively apathetic because they learn they are unable to change the situation. These stages are described by Bowlby as protest, despair and detachment. This sequence of events could ultimately lead to the state of learned-helplessness (Seligman, 1975), where a child feels powerless and unable to help themselves – an extremely powerful predictor of depression in later life. How much better now to prevent a child's life being 'damaged' by something which can so easily be resolved.

WHAT ARE THE IMPLICATIONS OF PSYCHOLOGICAL RESEARCH?

What can we draw from the knowledge gained by psychological research? Have the countless thousands of studies that have been undertaken over the years served any purpose? Some of the issues which have been addressed by psychology do have very serious implications for our lives, while others have very little real relevance. Perhaps one of the major implications is the fact that psychology could be seen to encourage the labelling of people. Labels, once applied, are very difficult to remove. The labels that we do apply to people may come from some form of categorisation or testing. For example, someone could be labelled as intelligent or stupid, mentally ill or 'normal', a type A or type B personality and so on. The biggest problem here comes from the possibility that the tests themselves may lack any sort of validity (as shown by the study on defining abnormality by Rosenhan in 1973 and Gould's 1982 paper on intelligence testing). The implications attached to such methods of labelling go without saying.

Let me give you an example of labelling that I'm sure you will be familiar with, even though it is not psychological in nature – the question of HIV. If someone is concerned that they may have contracted the HIV virus, and they go to their doctor for a test, the doctor is obliged to report the fact to any life assurance company who may be interested in insuring the life of that person, even if the test proved negative. This would immediately make the insurance company jump to the conclusion that the person was promiscuous, gay or an intravenous drug user; otherwise why would they have asked for a test? These assumptions might increase their potential for dying at an earlier age than expected, so the individual would be quoted a much higher premium, even though none of the assumptions might be true.

Now take a situation where a person has been treated for a minor psychological disorder such as a bout of reactive depression. If this was to be put on a job application or mentioned in a reference, the interviewer might jump to all sorts of conclusions – even if the person had only suffered one bout of reactive depression.

Another way of looking at the implications attached to psychology as a discipline is to look at the ideas of the behaviourist, J.B. Watson. He claimed that the main aim of psychology was to develop a method of predicting and therefore controlling man's reactions. If we can label and categorise people, then we can predict the way they will react and consequently find some method of controlling it. Although this sounds horrific, I don't believe that it was meant in quite the way that we might believe, although the outcome does suggest that we would lose our freedom of choice. Behaviourists believe that our behaviour is shaped by the environment in which we grow up. We learn from that environment how to react because we have had our behaviour reinforced in the form of praise and reward. Therefore if we are reacting inappropriately, we need to understand why it has occurred as it may not be our fault, and we need then to change the conditions to prevent the behaviour occurring again. The trouble is, first, this implies that we have no ability to think and make choices for ourselves but are purely a product of the environment. Secondly, who is to say what is the correct behaviour? Society may say that we ought to behave in a certain way, but who made society? Only men who may not have known any better!

If we accept that it is possible to categorise and label accurately, predict and control the behaviour of mankind, what would be the point unless the data is held for some purpose or other? Where would such information be held, who would have access to it, what would it be used for? It would be nice to think that it would be used to ensure that each of us reaches our maximum potential and as a means of enhancing our opportunities. However, some may argue that it is more likely (bearing in mind the financial implications) that this would not occur and it would instead be used as a way of restricting the freedom of choice we now have, as a means of social control by central government.

Perhaps the most frightening aspect of these arguments is that they are based on 'scientific evidence'. Psychology is a science, and if psychology claims that we can categorise people according to their abilities or weaknesses, then why not do so? If we can learn the skills to predict behaviour, then control of that behaviour must follow. You will probably have realised by now that although psychology is a form of natural science, there is one extra ingredient – man – that prevents it from being a purely objective science. Psychology is the study of mind and behaviour *by human beings* – therefore it cannot be purely objective. Surely that alone is enough to concern even the most committed behaviourist who tries to claim that psychologists always get it right.

Another implication of psychology is that if its theories can tell us what is 'normal', what happens when we can't achieve that ideal? I have a good general understanding of psychology and yet I don't fit the category of 'ideal' in many respects. I have the legacy of my upbringing to deal with, I have gone through periods of stress and depression and I doubt if I would make the top scores for intelligence. I would like to have a high degree of self-efficacy, be a stable extrovert, have an internal locus of control and so on. Because I understand that many of these concepts are no more than concepts, I don't feel like jumping off the nearest cliff, but on the other hand I often wish that I did fit into the 'ideal' category, in the belief that it would make life easier.

Psychology took giant leaps forward when the idea of information processing was suggested as a way of looking at the workings of the human brain. The idea that we could look at the brain as a processing system, similar to that of a computer, brought about the **cognitive revolution** beginning in the late 1950s. The problems that lay ahead for the researchers really related to the fact that the majority of 'human computers' seemed to have different processors, each with their own idiosyncratic components and this made it very hard to categorise all behaviours in the way that scientific proof required. This modern approach, with its focus on rules and laws and absolutes, has been superseded by the 'postmodernist' philosophy. This focuses on differences and diverse values which are affected by the situations and by personal experiences.

I think that this is where we should be today – not judging people by sets of rules which are not particularly relevant to them. We should use what we know to help understand and explain, and to try to improve our potential and alleviate the suffering which is often man's state. The implications of psychological research should therefore be seen as constructive rather than destructive, but can only be so as long as we don't forget that we, the researchers, are human, fallible, opinionated and often wrong!

How to put it all together!

9

- *Questions asking you to describe*
- *Questions asking you to evaluate*
- *Questions asking you to apply*

We have now covered the different ways of describing psychological studies. We have looked at how to explain the results using different perspectives. We have also looked at which areas to focus on in making an evaluation. Looking at all the possible methodological and ethical flaws that experiments are prone to may make you feel that no research is ever perfect or worthwhile. Well, don't forget, that is not actually the case. Perhaps I have been ultra-critical here and have come up with so many different weaknesses that can be found in psychological research that you are now reeling under the weight of potential problems. In reality, most studies have only one or two really relevant evaluative issues, and even then the researchers may well have been aware of them but may have decided that there was no other alternative way of conducting the study without introducing yet more problems.

You must also remember that many of the studies do have **positive issues** or **strengths** as well as weaknesses and it is essential that you take these into account.

Depending on the type of research, studies may have the following strengths:

- Researchers often match participants effectively. They may well counterbalance for order and fatigue effects.
- They may well conduct research in the same or matched environments.
- Their data collection techniques are often shared with other researchers so they end up with reliable results, for example in observational studies.

- They may take participants from different cultural groups.
- They may actually employ statisticians to analyse their data, which would obviously rule out any possible biases.
- They may use double blind techniques whereby the researcher cannot influence the participants in any way.
- They may conduct a longitudinal study to allow for the problems with snapshot studies, which simply capture the responses of participants at one moment in time.

and so on …

My final efforts here are intended to help you, the student, pull all this information together. To do so, I have divided this chapter into three parts by combining all the information to use when you are given an essay topic.

The OCR syllabus requires you to study two areas of applied psychology out of a choice of six. You will be asked to answer two questions from each area that you have studied (for example two from health and two from education – if these are the areas you have studied. The first question will involve describing and evaluating, the second will involve describing, evaluating and then applying what you know to a new situation. At the end of each of the sections in this chapter, I have given examples of questions taken from the OCR specimen papers (2000) which are relevant to that section. Within each subject area:

'you are required to answer one question from section A and one from section B'.

DESCRIBE THE KNOWLEDGE … • • • • • • • • • • • • • • • • •

First of all you need to look at the questions which begin by asking you to 'Describe what psychologists have found out about …'.

The format of this question may use the wording above, but the words 'Examine', 'Consider' or 'Outline' may also be used, as they all have similar meanings. There is no real distinction between these terms because they are all asking you for evidence in a reasonable amount of detail. The evidence you give can be in the form of studies, theories or even perspectives. The best way to address the question is to take some evidence (the amount required will depend on whether you are answering a question from Section A or Section B,) and then develop that evidence. This can be done in a number of ways; perhaps by giving details about how studies were undertaken or by providing explanations about the different theories you have mentioned, although it is acceptable to use more evidence and cover it in less detail.

You need to describe studies or theories which are directly related to the area about which you have been asked. The question may simply ask for one piece of evidence. On the other hand, it may not actually specify, so you need to make sure that you read the question carefully.

You must remember that you need to explain why the evidence or theory you have described actually happened. You can do this either from a specific perspective by using the different explanations, such as those based on social or developmental psychology, or by considering some other possible explanation.

Let me give you an example of how we would address a question's 'describe' element. Suppose the question asked you to 'describe what we have found out about doctor–patient communication'.

One of the studies we could use would be the study by Ley (1978), which investigated how much people remembered of their consultation and the requests of the doctor to carry out the treatment. In order to describe this study effectively, we would have to state an aim of the study, to describe the procedure, the findings and explain why the conclusions were drawn.

Describing the study:

Psychologists have found out that much of the information given to patients by their doctors is actually forgotten. To support this idea, one study conducted by Ley (1978) discovered that patients remembered only about 55 per cent of what their doctor had said to them. Ley asked people who had just visited their doctor to recall what the doctor had said to them and what he advised. In order to check how accurate they were and to estimate the percentage of information recalled, the information was compared with a record of what had actually been said to them. He also discovered that the mistakes they made were not random.

The findings plus explanations

- Ley discovered that the participants remembered the first thing they were told, which could be explained by the **primacy effect**, where we remember the first piece of information rather than information that is given to us at a later stage. The number of times the doctor repeated the information made no difference to recall. This could be explained by the fact that the patients may not have been deeply processing the later information for meaning (Craik and Lockhart, 1972) and therefore failed to store it in long-term memory. This idea was supported by the fact that patients who had some medical knowledge remembered more information. The information they were given would have more meaning to them than to the 'naïve' patients.

- Ley also discovered that patients remembered information which was put into categories, rather than information that was provided with no structure. This again links in with theories of memory and how we are more likely to remember information that has some kind of structure to give it meaning.

> • The results could also be explained by the fact that the participants may have
> been in a high level of autonomic arousal by the situation, and were more con-
> cerned with their discomfort at this increased level than the information they
> were being given.

If you look at Figures 1.6 and 1.7 in Chapter 1 (pages 10 and 11), this will help you make sure you have described and explained the information effectively.

As a revision guide, it might be worth finding yourself an A4 sheet of paper and making yourself brief notes under the following headings. You could then use either one of the studies or all of them, depending on the nature of the question.

Describe what psychologists have found out about ...
1 This first piece of evidence could be a study or a theory.
  • For theories: Describe the theory in some detail and then the evidence (if any) to back it up.
  • For studies: Describe the study including the aim of study, details about the study, and results.
  Then explain the findings
  • For theories: How they work.
  • For studies: How the results coud be explained.
2 This second piece of evidence could be a study or a theory
  Describe it ...
  then explain the findings ...
3 and
4 as above

To give you an idea of the kind of format the 'describe' part of the questions may take, I have listed different questions from both section A and section B of the OCR specimen papers (2000).

Note: You must be careful because although the **basic** skills are the same for both Section A and Section B questions, *the mark scheme is actually different*. Section B will give you more marks and therefore requires you to show more sophisticated psychological knowledge. If you spend time going into the same amount of detail with a Section A answer, you may find you are taking up too much of your exam time.

Section A: Marks available (6)

Section A may ask about **one or more** studies. Make sure you read the question carefully because if it asks for one study/theory then you must write about only one (even if you know about loads more and want to blind the examiner with your knowledge!) However, the question may not specify one, in which case the expectation would be that you write about more than one.

If you want to gain maximum marks for Section A you will be expected to focus your answer on the question. You have to provide an accurate, informed and thorough description. You have to give a detailed answer which is well-organised and well-expressed, to show that you understand what you have written.

Section B: Marks available (10)

Irrespective of the wording of the Section B question, you will be required to describe more than one study.

In Section B you are asked to show three things:

1 **Knowledge of concepts, terminology and quality of English** (*3 marks available for this subsection*)
   In order to get full marks for this section you have to present 'appropriate concepts from two (or more) theories or methods or perspectives/approaches and use impressive psychological terminology'. Spelling must be largely accurate (one or two errors are allowed) and you should show good sentence construction, clearly expressed views and appropriate punctuation.

2 **Evidence** (*4 marks available for this subsection*)
   In order to get full marks in this section, you need to have 'appropriate psychological evidence … accurately described that is wide-ranging in scope and detail'.

3 **Understanding** (*3 marks available for this subsection*)
   In order to get full marks in this section, you need to demonstrate 'explicitly applied understanding throughout' your answer. This means you must show that you really do understand what the studies show and this can be demonstrated by 'clarification of terminology, use of examples and by expanding on complex points'. The answer also has to be 'coherent and well-structured'.

In order to make your understanding explicit, you can use sentences such as 'what this evidence shows us in relation to the question is …'.

You must also remember to explain the terms you are using and to expand your explanation of any points which may seem complex, thus showing the examiner how much you know.

On the next page are the sample questions which ask you to 'describe' some psychological research from both Section A and Section B of the paper.

Educational Psychology

Section A

(a)   Describe one study of learning styles which uses a questionnaire as its form of measurement. [6]

or

(a)   Outline the **humanistic** approach to education. [6]

Section B

(a)   Describe what psychologists have discovered about the design and layout of classroom environments. [10]

or

(a)   Consider a number of ways in which educational performance is assessed in schools. [6]

Health Psychology

Section A

(a)   Describe one way in which pain has been assessed using the observation method. [6]

or

(a)   Consider one **physiological** explanation of pain. [6]

Section B

(a)   Describe what psychologists have learned about health promotion. [10]

or

(a)   Describe how psychologists explain why people do not adhere to medical requests. [6]

Organisational Psychology

Section A

(a)   Examine one case study of job analysis which uses questionnaires. [6]

or

(a)   Consider one **universalist** theory of leadership. [6]

Section B

(a)   Describe psychological evidence demonstrating the adverse effects of organisational work conditions and schedules. [10]

or

(a)   Describe a number of theories of motivation in the workplace. [6]

Environmental Psychology

Section A

(a) Outline one study of personal space in which 'invasions' of personal space were used to gather data. [6]

or

(a) Briefly discuss evidence which claims high temperature causes aggression. [6]

Section B

(a) Describe psychological evidence which demonstrates the effects of 'crowding' on human behaviour. [10]

or

(a) Explain what psychologists have found out about territory. [6]

Sport Psychology

Section A

(a) Examine one theory which explains why sportspeople are aggressive. [6]

or

(a) Describe one way in which attentional focus has been measured using the self-report. [6]

Section B

(a) Describe what psychologists have learned about arousal and sport performance. [10]

or

(a) Examine what psychologists have learned about the effects of an audience on human performers. [6]

Criminal Psychology

Section A

(a) Describe one laboratory study of eyewitness testimony. [6]

or

(a) Describe one study which demonstrates the development of moral and legal judgement in children. [6]

Section B

(a) Describe jury decision-making processes. [10]

or

(a) Consider psychological studies of offender profiling. [6]

EVALUATE THE KNOWLEDGE ... • • • • • • • • • • • • • • • •

Next you need to look at a question which begins by asking you to 'Evaluate what psychologists have found out about ...'. As with the first section another phrase may be used such as 'Compare and contrast ...' or 'Discuss the strengths and weaknesses ...' but again they mean the same thing. There are a total of 16 marks available for evaluation which should make you realise how important it is to evaluate effectively.

Marks are awarded for:

- **Evaluation issues** (*three marks available for this subsection – one for each issue*)
  In order to get full marks, you really need to provide *three* good 'meaty' issues and explain what you mean by them – one mark for each issue.
- **Evaluation evidence** – for each issue (*six marks available for this subsection – two for each issue*)
  In order to get full marks you need to provide two (or more) pieces of appropriate psychological evidence for *each* issue you have mentioned above. This means that you must produce evidence to illustrate the point you are making rather than just saying for example, the study by so-and-so was 'useful'. If you have only thought of two evaluation issues, you can only get four marks in this section.
- **Analysis cross-referencing** – for all issues (*three marks available for this subsection*)
  This means comparing and contrasting on all three issues in order to get full marks. The comparisons and contrasts have to be evident throughout the answer and must be accurate, detailed and effective.
- **Analysis structure and argument** – for all issues (*six marks available for this subsection*)
  This means making sure the evaluation section reads well and makes sense and that the argument is clearly stated and understandable. In order to get full marks you must make sure that your arguments demonstrate originality and insight – that means that you must have thought the issues through for yourself and be able to demonstrate that you really understand what they mean.

If we continue with the Ley example, then you might say that as an evaluation it is very **useful** because it gives us an insight into an important everyday behaviour and can influence the way that we deal with situations in the future. It shows us that information that is given may not actually be remembered and therefore will not be acted upon. The study also has **ecological validity** because the study was conducted at doctors' surgeries and dealt with real consultations and the findings are likely to occur again in similar settings. The study is also **replicable** because the information given by doctors was recorded and used to contrast with what the patients thought they were hearing. The difference between the quantity of information given and received could be measured. On the other hand, you might comment that the crucial issue is whether people then act on the information; even if they remember what the doctor said they might not do anything about it. Therefore we need to take the research a step further to look at what people actually do.

There are so many issues you could use to evaluate. Look at Figures 1.6 and 1.7 in Chapter 1 (pages 10 and 11) and this will help you make sure you have evaluated the information effectively and should help you to answer the questions you may be asked.

Below are four main issues you could use for evaluation (although you actually need only three). It might be worth trying to make one point under each of the headings appropriate to your answer. If you manage to do this, you will be demonstrating breadth in your knowledge rather than just reciting a long list of repetitive and trivial points. (**Note:** it is often very tempting to look at the methodology alone, but this will lose marks.)

a) **Theory – does the research actually relate to theory that was being investigated?**
   - Is the research a valid measure of the theoretical concept under investigation?
   - Also, how was the variable measured (e.g. if the researchers were interested in looking at 'disruptive behaviour', how did they define disruption?)
b) **Methods – how did the researchers collect and analyse the data?**
   Were there any sources of bias?
   - Was the sample representative?
   - Was there any experimenter bias?
   - Did the participants show demand characteristics?
   - Was the methodology culturally biased?
   Were there any sources of error?
   - Was the procedure transparent?
     - Were there any problems with data measurement or collection?
     - Were the measurements valid?
   - Was the study reliable?
   - Did the participants show demand characteristics?
   Were there problems with interpretation of the results?
   - Was the data misinterpreted?
   - Does the study have ecological validity?
c) **Ethics**
   Did the researchers follow ethical guidelines?
d) **Usefulness**
   - Is the study useful? Does it contribute to human welfare and understanding? What are the implications we can draw from the study?
   - Are the results of the study out of date?

Again you might find it worth using another sheet of A4 paper to make brief evaluation notes relating to the studies you have described in the first section to use as a further guide to revision. Don't forget you need to compare and contrast issues where possible and make sure they are accurate, detailed and effective. Remember: you need to identify the issue, say whether it is a strength or weakness in the studies you described earlier, and then see if any of the other studies you have described have the same strengths or weaknesses, or possibly different ones.

Evaluate what psychologists have found out about ...
(Fill in at least three sections)

1   The first evaluative issue could address whether the research you have described really relates to the theories being investigated.
- Does the research really measure the concepts under investigation?
- How were the variables measured? Were they valid measurements?
  - i   For study one*
  - ii   For study two
  - iii For study three*

(* can be compared to each other and contrasted with the unstarred item.)

Note: If you have talked about a theory (or a number of theories) in section A, you could actually evaluate the fact that there may be limited or no evidence to back up the theory and that the behaviour could perhaps be explained by another theory/method/perspective or approach.

2   The second evaluative issue could address an issue related to the methods used by the researchers and how they collected and analysed the data.
- Were there any sources of bias in any of the studies?
- Were there any sources of error in any of the studies?
- Were there problems with interpretation of the results in any of the studies?
  - i   For study one*
  - ii   For study two*
  - ii   For study three

(* can be compared to each other and contrasted with the unstarred item.)

3   The third evaluative issue could address the issue of ethics.
- Did the researchers follow ethical guidelines in all of the studies you have described?
  - i   For study one
  - ii   For study two*
  - iii For study three*

(* can all be compared to each other.)

4   The fourth evaluative issue questions whether the research was useful.
   • Is the research useful? Does it contribute to human welfare and under-standing?
   • What are the implications of the study (if any)?
   • Are the results of the study out of date?
      i   For study one
      ii For study two
      ii For study three
(They can all be contrasted with each other.)

Below I have listed the 'evaluate' part of the different questions taken from the OCR specimen papers (2000).

Educational Psychology
Section A
(b) Discuss the strengths and weaknesses of alternative methodologies to measure learning styles. [10]

or

(b) Compare and contrast **humanistic** with other explanations of education. [10]
Section B
(b) Evaluate what psychologists have discovered about the design and layout of classroom environments. [16]

or

(b) Evaluate the assessments of educational performance given in part (a). [16]

Health Psychology
Section A
(b) Compare and contrast the use of the observation method to measure pain with alternative methodologies. [10]

or

(b) Compare and contrast **physiological** with alternative theories of pain. [10]
Section B
(b) Discuss what psychologists have learned about health promotion. [16]

or

(b) Discuss how psychologists explain non-adherence to medical requests. [16]

Organisational Psychology

Section A

(b) Assess the extent to which results from the use of questionnaires in organisations can be generalised. [10]

or

(b) Discuss the extent to which **universalist** theories of leadership are reductionist. [10]

Section B

(b) Evaluate psychological evidence on the adverse effects of organisational work conditions and schedules. [16]

or

(b) Evaluate theories of motivation in the workplace. [16]

Environmental Psychology

Section A

(b) Discuss the ethics of studying personal space where 'invasions' of personal space are used. [10]

or

(b) Discuss the deterministic view that high temperature causes aggression. [10]

Section B

(b) Evaluate psychological evidence which demonstrates the effects of 'crowding' on human behaviour. [16]

or

(b) Discuss what psychologists have found out about territory. [16]

Sport Psychology

Section A

(b) Compare and contrast the theory described in part (a) as to why sportspeople are aggressive with alternative approaches. [10]

or

(b) Discuss the use of alternative methodologies to study 'attentional focus'. [10]

Section B

(b) Evaluate what psychologists have learned about arousal and sport performance. [16]

or

(b) Evaluate what psychologists have found out about the effects of an audience on human performers. [16]

Criminal Psychology

Section A

(b)   Compare and contrast the laboratory method to study eyewitness testimony with one alternative method. [10]

or

(b)   Discuss the use of children in psychological studies of crime. [10]

Section B

(b   Discuss jury decision-making processes. [16]

or

(b)   Evaluate psychological studies of offender profiling. [16]

APPLY THE KNOWLEDGE ...●●●●●●●●●●●●●●●●●●●●●●●

Finally you need to look at how the psychological findings you have studied can be applied to a practical situation. After all, what is the point of studying psychology unless it has some kind of practical application? The question you will have to address may involve the description of a situation or the outline of a specific problem that needs to be addressed. This area really relates back to the section on the usefulness of the studies that you have covered. The other thing to remember here is that many of the areas you have considered during the course of your study could apply to any area of psychology.

In the last chapter I gave a couple of examples of how past research does have some practical and relevant applications in the real world. The work of Elizabeth Loftus and John Bowlby was influential in changing policy, within the legal system and within the health service respectively. We are now going to look at how we can apply past research to new and novel situations which might seem to have little relationship with the original studies.

All students of psychology will encounter the work of Milgram and Zimbardo over the course of their studies. Other familiar studies may come from the area of children's development such as the work of Piaget on cognitive development or Bandura (1961) on aggression. We have already discussed the fact that the early studies may still have a relevance today and the same findings may well occur – but how do we transfer the information gathered from say, a laboratory study, to a real-life situation?

First of all, look at the task ahead of you and think of everything you know about the situation:

Take, for example, the following question from health psychology:

Using your knowledge of health promotion, suggest a programme that would encourage children to eat in healthier ways.

Here is a very brief summary of the way you could go about looking at the situation. **First of all, decide what you know about promoting health:**

- Do you want to frighten them? (Janis and Feshbach, 1953)
- How about using the Yale Model of Communication which says:
    - You need to have a credible source of information.
    - You need to have a clear message which is one-sided if the targets are young children, but two-sided if they are older and are not generally sympathetic to the argument.
    - You need to consider the medium to be used, e.g. television or radio, magazines, etc.
- You also need to think about where the children are going to be when they are given the message.

Secondly, you need to think about how to make children behave in certain ways:

- Children tend to conform to group norms (Asch, 1951).
- They also like to feel part of a group, and are more likely to favour that group if it is seen to be in competition with another group (Tajfel, 1970).
- They may well respond to a legitimate authority figure (Milgram, 1963).
- Most of all, if their behaviour is reinforced they are more likely to continue to behave in that way (Skinner, 1938).
- And if they see others doing it, especially if the others are 'significant', they will copy them (Bandura, 1961).

If you are sure you really understand how these theories work then it shouldn't be very difficult to come up with some kind of suggestion for a programme to encourage children to eat in healthier ways. At this point:

- you have a suggestion;
- a theory on which it is based;
- an explanation of how it would work;
- and finally, an idea of what would be the likely effect of such a programme (evaluate its effectiveness).

There are eight marks available in this application section. In order to gain full marks you need to look at the number of suggestions the question requires. If the question does not specify a particular number, you must use **two** or more suggestions. You must make them 'appropriate to the assessment request, base them on appropriate psychological evidence' and make sure they are 'detailed and clearly explained'. You must also make sure that 'the relationship between the evidence and the suggestion is apparent' for any suggestion you make. Finally the answer should include 'explicitly applied understanding throughout', that means you must show that you really understand the way your suggestion would affect the problem. You must also explain any terminology you use, give examples of how the suggestion could be implemented and how it should work, expand on any complex points (not simply assume that the examiner will understand what you mean) and last of all make sure that what you write is 'coherent and well-structured'.

One of the ways of doing it is again to make A4 revision sheets. On the sheet you could suggest a number of ways of addressing issues you have covered during your studies, outline the evidence on which they are based, and finally explain why they should work. I have used an example taken from **environmental psychology**, which focuses on the practical use of information on territorial boundaries. Note that this particular question requires two pieces of practical information whereas the exam paper may specify a different number.

> **Apply your knowledge of psychology to the following situation:**
> Suggest two ways in which a householder can make their property more secure against burglary
> **First suggestion:**
> Studies on which it is based:
> Explanation of how the suggestion would work:
> **Second suggestion:**
> Studies on which it is based:
> Explanation of how the suggestion would work:

Below I have listed the 'applied' part of the different questions taken from the OCR specimen papers (2000). Choosing the options that you are currently studying, try doing the same for each of these applied questions.

> **Educational Psychology**
> **Section B**
> (c) Giving reasons for your answer, suggest a number of design features a 'perfect' classroom would have to maximise educational performance. [8]
>
> *or*
>
> (c) Giving reasons for your answer, suggest ONE way to assess children doing Key Stage 1 science. [8]

Health Psychology

Section B

(c) Using your knowledge of health promotion, suggest a programme that would encourage children to eat in healthier ways. [8]

or

(c) Suggest two ways in which adherence to medical requests may be improved. Give reasons for your answer. [8]

Organisational Psychology

Section B

(c) Suggest two ways in which temporal work conditions may be organised to minimise potentially adverse effects. [8]

or

(c) Giving reasons for your answer, suggest motivators that could be used to increase sales targets for salespeople in your company. [8]

Environmental Psychology

Section B

(c) Based on the evidence you have presented above (*evidence demonstrating the effects of 'crowding'*), suggest ways in which psychologists can eliminate the effects of 'crowding'. [8]

or

(c) Using your psychological knowledge, suggest two ways in which a householder can make their property more secure against burglary. [8]

Sport Psychology

Section B

(c) Using your psychological knowledge, suggest an 'anxiety management' technique that could be used by an athlete to improve performance. [8]

or

(c) Suggest two reasons why teams often have an advantage when 'playing at home'. [8]

(**Note**: *Although this is a slightly different format, it is asking you to use the knowledge you have about audience effects on a specific situation.*)

Criminal Psychology

Section B

(c) If you were a member of a jury, suggest what rules you may make for yourself to prevent you from making the wrong decision. Give reasons for your answer. [8]

or

(c) Suggest what the aims of offender profiling should be. Give reasons for your answer. [8]

Don't forget, more than anything else, you must give the examiner the opportunity to see what you know, but examiners aren't interested in everything, only the bits that relate to the questions they have asked. Read the questions two or three times if necessary and make sure you really understand what they are asking of you. Answer the questions in any order, starting with the one you feel you know the best. This will make you feel more confident and hopefully more relaxed – after all, you think more clearly when you aren't over-aroused! Make sure you watch the clock and divide your time equally between questions. You can always go back and write some more at the end of an earlier question if you have time at the end.

And finally, good luck …

Bibliography

Ainsworth, M.D.S., Blehar, M.C., Waters, E. and Wall, S. (1978) *Patterns of Attachment*. Hillsdale, J.J.: Erlbaum.

Allport, D.A., Antonis, B. and Reynolds, P. (1972) On the division of attention: A disproof of the single channel hypothesis. *Quarterly Journal of Experimental Psychology*, 24, 225–235.

Altman, I. (1975) *The Environment and Social Behaviour*. Monterey, CA: Brooks/Cole.

Aronson, E., Wilson, T.D. and Akert, R.M. (1999) *Social Psychology* (3rd edition). New York: Longman.

Asch, S.E. (1951) Effect of group pressure upon the modification and distortion of judgements. In H. Guetzkow (Ed), *Groups, Leadership and Men*. Pittsburg, Pennsylvania: Carnegie Press.

Atkinson, R.C. and Shiffrin, R.M. (1968) Human memory: a proposed system and its control processes. In K.W. Spence and J.T. Spence (Eds), *The Psychology of Learning and Motivation 2*. London: Academic Press.

Bandura, A. and Walters, R. (1963) *Social Learning and Personality Development*. New York: Holt, Rinehart & Winston.

Bandura, A., Ross, D. and Ross, S.A. (1961) Transmission of aggression through imitation of aggressive models. *Journal of Abnormal and Social Psychology*, 63, 575–82.

Banyard, P. (1996) *Applying Psychology to Health*. London: Hodder & Stoughton.

Banyard, P. (1996) *Introducing Psychological Research*. London: Macmillan Press.

Banyard, P. and Hayes, N. (1994) *Psychology Theory and Application*. London: Chapman & Hall.

Barefoot, J.C., Hoople, H. and McClay, D. (1972) Avoidance of an act which would violate personal space. *Psychonomic Science*, 28, 205–206.

Baron-Cohen, S., Leslie, A.M. and Frith, U. (1985) Does the autistic child have a 'theory of mind'? *Cognition*, 21, 37–46.

Bartlett, F.C. (1932) *Remembering: A Study in Experimental and Social Psychology*. Cambridge: Cambridge University Press.

Barton, J., Chassin, L., Presson, C.C. and Sherman, S.J. (1982) Social image factors as motivators of smoking initiation in early and middle adolescence. *Child Development*, 53, 1499–1511.

Bernstein, B. (1961) Social class and linguistic development. In A.H. Halsey, J. Flaud and C.A. Anderson (Eds), *Education, Economy and Society*. London: Collier-Macmillan Ltd.

Bernstein, B. (1973) *Class, Codes and Control*. London: Paladin.

Bowlby J. (1953) *Childcare and the Growth of Love*. Penguin Books.

Broadbent, D.E. (1958) *Perception and Communication*. Oxford: Pergamon.

Brophy, J. and Good, T. (1970) Teachers' communication of differential expectations for children's performances: some behavioural data. *Journal of Educational Psychology*, 61, 365–374.

Browne, K.D. and Pennell, A.E. (1997) Film violence and young offenders. *Aggression and Violent Behaviour*, 3, 27–35.

Brunswik, E. (1956) *Perception and the Representative Design of Psychological Experiments*. Berkeley: University of California Press.

Brunswik, E. (1959) The conceptual framework of psychology. In O. Neurath, R. Camp and C. Morris (Eds), *Foundation of the Unity of Science: Towards an International Encyclopaedia of Unified Science*. Chicago: University of Chicago Press.

Buchanan, D. and Huczynski, A. (1997) *Organisational Behaviour: An Introductory Text* (3rd edition). London: Prentice Hall.

Bulpitt, C. (1988) in R.M. Kaplan, J.F. Sallis and T.L. Patternson (1993) *Health and Human Behaviour*. New York: McGraw-Hill.

Burns, G. (1985) *Somebody's Husband, Somebody's Son*. London: Pan.

Campbell, D.T. and Stanley, J.C. (1966) *Experimental and Quasi-experimental Designs for Research*. Chicago: Rand McNally.

Carlsmith, J., Ellsworth, P. and Aronson, E. (1976) *Methods of Research in Social Psychology*. Reading, MA: Addison-Wesley.

Cave, S. (1998) *Applying Psychology to the Environment*. London: Hodder & Stoughton.

Charlton, T. (2000) http://www.chelt.ac.uk/ess/st-helena/res.htm

Clark, K. and Clark, M. (1939) The development of consciousness of self in the emergence of racial identification in Negro pre-school children. *Journal of Social Psychology*, 10, 591–597.

Cohen, S., Glass, D.C. and Singer, J.E. (1973) Apartment noise, auditory discrimination and reading ability in children. *Journal of Experimental Social Psychology*, 9, 407–422.

Cook, M. (1970) Experiments on orientation and proxemics. *Human Relations*, 23, 61–76.

Coolican, H. (1994) *Research Methods and Statistics in Psychology*. London: Hodder & Stoughton.

Cotterell, N.B. (1968) Performance in the presence of other human beings: mere presence, audience and affiliation effects. In E.C. Simmell, R.A. Hoppe and G.A. Milton (Eds), *Social Facilitation and Imitative Behaviour*. Boston: Allyn and Bacon.

Craik F.I.M. and Lockhart R. (1972) Levels of processing. *Journal of Verbal Behaviour*, 11 671–684.

Curtiss, S. (1977) *Genie: A Psycholinguistic Study of a Modern-day 'Wild Child'*. London: Academic Press.

Davis, A. (1983) Contextual sensitivity in young children's drawings. *Journal of Experimental Child Psychology*, 35, 478–86.

Dement W. and Kleitman N. (1957) The relation of eye movements during sleep to dream activity: an objective method for the study of dreaming. *Journal of Experimental Psychology*, 53, 339–46.

Deregowski,. B. (1972) Pictorial perception and culture. *Scientific American*, 227, 82–88.

Donnerstein, E. and Wilson, D.W. (1976). Effects of noise and perceived control on ongoing and subsequent aggressive behaviour. *Journal of Personality and Social Psychology*, 34, 774–781.

Eysenck, H.J. (1947) *Dimensions of personality*. London: Routledge and Kegan Paul.

Fallon, A.E. and Rozin, P. (1985) Sex differences in perceptions of desirable body shape. *Journal of Abnormal Psychology*, 94, 102–105.

Feldman, S.D. (1971) *The presentation of shortness in everyday life – height and heightism in American society: towards a sociology of stature*. Paper presented before the meetings of the American Sociological Association, cited in E. Berschield and E. Walster (1974) *op. cit.*

Feshback, S. and Singer, R.D. (1971) *Television and Aggression: An Experimental Field Study*. San Francisco: Jossey-Bass.

Festinger, L. and Carlsmith, L.M. (1959) Cognitive consequences of forced compliance. *Journal of Abnormal and Social Psychology* 58, 3–10.

Fiedler, F.E. (1967) *A Theory of Leadership Effectiveness*. New York: McGraw-Hill.

Freud, S. (1901/1976) *The Psychopathology of Everyday Life*. Pelican Freud Library (5). Harmondsworth: Penguin.

Freud, S. (1909/1977) *Analysis of a Phobia in a Five-year-old Boy*. Pelican Freud Library (8). *Case Histories 1*, 169–306. Harmondsworth: Penguin.

Galton, F. (1884) *Hereditary Genius*. New York: Appleton.

Gibson, J.J. (1966) *The Senses Considered as Perceptual Systems*. Boston: Houghton Mifflin.

Gould, S.J. (1982) A nation of morons. *New Scientist,* 6 May, 349–352.

Green, P. (1985) Multi-ethnic teaching and the pupil's self-concept. In *DES Education for All*. London: HMSO.

Gregory, R. (1973) The confounded eye. In R.L. Gregory and E.H. Gombrich (Eds), *Illusion in Nature and Art*. London: Duckworth.

Gross. R.D. (1992) *Psychology: Science of Mind and Behaviour* (2nd edition). London: Hodder & Stoughton.

Haney, C., Banks, W.C. and Zimbardo, P.G. (1973) A study of prisoners and guards in a simulated prison. *Naval Research Review*, 30, 4–17.

Harrower, J. (1998) *Applying Psychology to Crime*. London: Hodder & Stoughton.

Hayward, S. (1996) *Applying Psychology to Organisations*. London: Hodder & Stoughton.

Hinton, P.R. (1993) *The Psychology of Interpersonal Perception*. London: Routledge.

Hodges, J. and Tizard, B. (1989) Social and family relationships of ex-institutional adolescents. *Journal of Child Psychology and Psychiatry*, 30, 77–97.

Hofling, K.C., Brotzman, E., Dalrymple, S., Graves, N. and Pieces, C.M. (1966) An experimental study in the nurse–physician relationshp. *Journal of Nervous and Mental Disorders*, 143, 171–180.

Holmes, T.H. and Rahe, R.H. (1967) The social readjustment rating scale. *Journal of Psychosomatic Research*, 11, 213–218.

Horowitz, I.A. (1969) Effects of volunteering, fear arousal and number of communications on attitude change. *Journal of Personality and Social Psychology*, 11, 34–37.

Hraba, J. and Grant, G. (1970) Black is beautiful: a re-examination of racial preference and identification. *Journal of Personality and Social Psychology*, 16, 398–402.

Hughes, M. (1989) The child as learner: the contrasting views of developmental psychology and early education. In C. Desforges (Ed) Early Childhood Education: *British Journal of Educational Psychology Monograph Series No. 4*. Edinburgh: Scottish Academic Press.

Hurlock, E.B. (1925) An evaluation of certain incentives used in school work. *Journal of Educational Psychology*, 16, 145–159.

Janis, I. and Feshbach, S. (1953) Effects of fear-arousing communications. *Journal of Abnormal and Social Psychology*, 48, 78–92.

Kanner, A.D., Coynes, J.C., Schaefer, C. and Lazarus, R.S. (1981) Comparison of two modes of stress measurement: daily hassles and uplifts versus major life events. *Journal of Behavioural Medicine*, 4, 1–39.

Kaplan, R.M., Sallis, J.F. and Patterson, T.L. (1993) *Health and Human Behaviour*. New York: McGraw-Hill.

Kimmell, A.J. (1996) *Ethical Issues in Behavioural Research, a Survey*. Oxford: Blackwell.

Kretschmer, E. (1925) *Physique and Character*. New York: Harcourt Brace.

Lehrman, S. (1998) *DNA & Behavior. Is Our Fate in Our Genes?* www.dnafiles.org/about/pgm2/topic.html

Lerner, M.J. and Lichtman, R.R. (1968) Effects of perceived norms on attitudes and altruistic behaviour towards a dependent other. *Journal of Personality and Social Psychology*, 9, 226–232.

LeVay, S. and Hammer, D.H. (1994) Evidence for a biological influence in male homosexuality. *Scientific American*, May, 20–25.

Leventhal, H., Prohaska, T.R. and Hirschman, R.S. (1985) Preventive health behaviour across the life span. In J.C. Rosen and L.J. Solomon (Eds), *Prevention in Health Psychology*. Hanover, NH: University Press of New England.

Levine, J.D., Gordon, N.C. and Fields, H.L. (1978) The mechanism of placebo analgesia. *Lancet*, 23 September 654–657.

Ley, P. (1978) Memory for medical information. *British Journal of Social and Clinical psychology*, 18, 2, 245–255.

Loftus, E. (1979) Reactions to blatantly contradictory information. *Memory and Cognition*, 7, 368–374.

Loftus, E.F. and Palmer, J.J. (1974) Reconstruction of automobile destruction: an example of the interaction between language and memory. *Journal of Verbal Learning and Verbal Behaviour*, 13, 585–589.

Loftus, E.F., Loftus, G.R. and Messo, J. (1987). Some facts about 'weapon focus'. *Law and Human Behavior*, 11, 55–62.

Lowenthal, K.M. (2001) *An Introduction to Psychological Tests and Scales* (2nd edition). Hove: Psychology Press.

Luparello, T.J., Lyons, H.A., Bleecker, E.R. and Mcfadden, E.R. (1968) Influences of suggestion on airway reactivity in asthmatic subjects. *Psychosomatic Medicine*, 30, 819–825.

Mackworth, N.H. (1950) Researches on the measurement of human performance. *Medical Research Council Special Report*, 268, HMSO: London.

Mahoney, B. and Dixon, J. (1997) A fair and just system. *Psychology Review*, November, 30–32.

Marr, D. (1982) *Vision*. San Francisco: W.H. Freeman.

Mathews, K.E. and Canon, L.K. (1975) Environmental noise level as a determinant of helping behaviour. *Journal of Psychology*, 41, 247–254.

Mbiti, J.S. (1970) *African Religions and Philosophy*. New York: Doubleday.

McInerney, J. and Rothstein, M. (2001) *What implications does behavioural genetics have for society?* www.ornl.gov/hgmis/elsi/behavior.html

McInerney, J. D. (1999) Genes and behaviour: a complex relationship. *Judicature,* 83, 3, 112. Also found at http://www.ornl.gov/hgmis/publicat/judicature/article4.html

McKeever, W.F. (2000) A new family handedness sample with findings consistent with X-linked transmission. *British Journal of Psychology*, 91, 21–40.

McKennell, A.C. and Bynner, J.M. (1969) Self images and smoking behaviour among school boys. *British Journal of Educational Psychology*, 39, 27–39.

McKinlay, J.B. (1975) Who is really ignorant – physician or patient? *Journal of Health and Social Behaviour*, 16, 3–11.

McKinstry, B. and Wang, J. (1991) Putting on the style: what patients think of the way their doctor dresses. *British Journal of General Practice*, 41, 275–278.

McNicholas, J. and Collis, G.M. (2000) Dogs as catalysts for social interactions: robustness of the effect, *British Journal of Psychology*, 91, 61–70.

Melzack, R. (1975) The McGill Pain Questionnaire: major properties and scoring methods. *Pain*, 1, 277–299.

Michaels, J.W., Blommel, J.M., Brocato, R.M., Linkous, R.A., & Rowe, J.S. (1982). Social facilitation and inhibition in natural setting. *Replications in Social Psychology*, 2, 21–24.

Middlemist, D., Knowles, E.S. and Matter, C.F. (1976) Personal space invations in the laboratory. Suggestive evidence for arousal. *Journal of Persoanlity and Social Psychology*, 33, 541–546.

Milgram, S. (1963) Behavioural study of obedience. *Journal of Abnormal & Social Psychology*, 67, 371–378.

Minturn, A.L. and Bruner, J.S. In C.B. Dobson, M. Hardy, S. Heyes, A. Humphreys and P. Humphreys (1993) *Understanding Psychology*. London: Weidenfeld and Nicolson.

Nisbett, R.E., Caputo, C., Legant, P. and Marecek J. (1973) Behaviour as seen by the actor and as seen by the observer. *Journal of Personality and Social Psychology*, 27, 154–65.

Orne, M.T. (1959) The nature of hypnosis: artifact and essence. *Journal of Abnormal and Social Psychology*, 58, 277–299.

Orne, M.T. (1962) On the social psychology of the psychological experiment; with particular reference to demand characteristics and their implications. *American Psychologist*, 17, 776–783.

Pomerleau, O.F. and Pomerleau, C.S. (1989). 'A biobehavioural perspective on smoking.' In T. Ney and A. Gale (Eds). *Smoking and Human Behaviour*. New York: Wiley.

Patrinos, A. and Drell, D.W. (1997) Introducing the Human Genome Project: its relevance, triumphs and challenges. *The Judges' Journal of the American Bar Association*, 36, 3.

Patterson, M.L. and Holmes, D.S. (1966) Social interaction correlates of MMPI extraversion–introversion scale. *American Psychologist*, 21, 724–725.

Pavlov, I.P. (1927) *Conditioned Reflexes.* London: Oxford University Press.

Pfeifer, J.E. and Ogloff, J.R. (1991) Ambiguity and guilt determinations: a modern racism perspective. *Journal of Applied Social Psychology,* 21, 1713–1725.

Piaget, J. and Inhelder, B. (1956) *The Child's Conception of Space.* London: Routledge and Kegan Paul.

Piliavin, I.M., Rodin, J.A. and Piliavin, J. (1969) Good samaritanism: an underground phenomenon? *Journal of Personality and Social Psychology,* 13, 289–299.

Plomin, R. (1990) *Nature and Nurture.* Pacific Grove: Brooks/Cole.

Poulton, E.C., Hunt, J.C.R., Mumford, J.C. and Poulton, J. (1975) Mechanical disturbance produced by steady and gusty winds of moderate strength: skilled performance and semantic assessments. *Ergonomics,* 18, 651–673.

Raine, A., Buchsbaum, M. and LaCasse, L. (1997) Brain abnormalities in murderers indicated by positron emission tomography. *Biological Psychiatry 1997,* 42, 495–508.

Robinson, R. and West, R. (1992) A comparison of computer and questionnaire methods of history-taking in a genito-urinary clinic. *Psychology and Health,* 6, 77–84.

Rosenhan, D.L. (1973) On being sane in insane places. *Science,* 179, 250–258.

Rosenthal, R. and Fode K.L. (1963) The effects of experimenter bias on the performance of the albino rat. *Behavioural Science,* 8, 183–189.

Rosenthal, R. and Jacobson, L. (1968) *Pygmalion in the Classroom: Teachers' Expectations and Pupils' Intellectual Development.* New York: Holt, Rinehart and Winston.

Rosenthal, R. and Rosnow, R.L. (1975) *The Volunteer Subject.* New York: Wiley.

Rosenthal, R. and Rosnow, R.L. (1991) *Essentials of Behavioural Research: Methods and Data Analysis* (2nd edition). New York: McGraw–Hill.

Roter, D.L. and Hall, J.A. (1987) Physicians; interviewing styles and medical information obtained from patients. *Journal of General Internal Medicine,* 2, 325–329.

Roth, D.L. and Holmes, D.S. (1985) Influence of physical fitness in determining the impact of stressful life events on physical and psychological health. *Psychosomatic Medicine,* 47, 164–173.

Ruback, R.B. and Pandey, J. (1992) Very hot and really crowded: Quasi-experimental investigations of Indian 'Tempos'. *Environment and Behaviour,* 24, 527–554.

Ruble, D.N. (1977) Premenstrual symptoms. A reinterpretation. *Science,* 197, 291–292.

Ryckman, R.M., Robbins, M.A., Kaczor, L.M. and Gold, J.A. (1989) Male and female raters' stereotyping of male and female physiques. *Personality and Social Psychology Bulletin,* 15, 244–251.

Sapir, E. (1947) *Selected Writings in Language, Culture and Personality.* Los Angeles: University of California Press.

Sarafino, E. (1994) *Health Psychology: Biopsychosocial Interactions* (2nd edition). New York: Wiley.

Schachter, S. and Singer, J.E. (1962) Cognitive, social and physiological determinants of emotional state. *Psychological Review,* 69, 5, 379–399.

Schachter, S., Silverstein, B., Kozlowski, L.T., Perlick, D., Herman, C.P. and Liebling, B. (1977) Studies of the interaction of psychological and pharmacological determinants of smoking. *Journal of Experimental Psychology: General,* 106, 3–40.

Schwartz, B. and Barsky, S.F. (1977) The home advantage. *Social Forces*, 55, 641–661.

Sears, D.O. (1986) College sophomores in the laboratory: influences of a narrow data base on psychology's view of human nature. *Journal of Personality and Social Psychology*, 51, 515–530.

Seligman, M.E.P. (1975) *Helplessness: On Depression, Development and Death*. San Francisco: Freeman.

Severson, H.H. and Lichtenstein, E. (1986). Smoking prevention programs for adolescents: rationale and review. In N.A. Krasnegor, J.D. Arasteh and M.F. Cataldo (Eds), *Child Health Behaviour: A Behavioural Pediatrics Perspective*. New York: Wiley.

Shaffer, L.H. (1975) Multiple attention in continuous verbal tasks. In P.M.A. Rabbitt and S. Dornic (Eds). *Attention and Performance* (Volume V). London: Academic Press.

Sheldon, W.H. (1954) *Atlas of Men: A Guide for Somatotyping the Human Male at all Ages*. New York: Harper and Row.

Sherif, M. (1956) *Experiments in Group Conflict*. Harper & Row.

Shiffrin, R.M. and Schneider, W. (1977) Controlled and automatic human information processing II: perceptual learning, automatic attending and a general theory. *Psychological Review*, 84, 127–190.

Skinner, B.F. (1938) *The Behaviour of Organisms*. New York: Appleton-Century-Crofts.

Sommer, R. (1969) *Personal Space*. Englewood Cliffs, NJ: Prentice Hall.

Sperry, R.W. (1968) Hemisphere deconnection and unity in conscious awareness. *American Psychologist*, 23, 723–733.

Stone, G.L. and Morden, C.J. (1976) Effect of distance on verbal productivity. *Journal of Counselling Psychology*, 23, 486–488.

Swigonski, M.E. (1987) Bio-psycho-social factors affecting coping and compliance with the hemodialysis treatment regimen. *University Microfilms International*, (Order No. 8803518).

Tajfel, H. (1970) Experiments in intergroup discrimination. *Scientific American*, 223, 96–102.

Thibaut, J.W. and Kelley, H.H. (1959) *The Social Psychology of Groups*. New York: Wiley.

Thigpen, C.H. and Cleckley, H. (1954) A case of multiple personality. *Journal of Abnormal and Social Psychology*, 49, 135–151.

Tinbergen, N. (1952) The curious behaviour of the stickleback. *Scientific American*, 187, 22–26.

Tipples, J. and Sharma, D. (2000) Facial distinctiveness: its measurement, distribution and influence on immediate and delayed recognition. *British Journal of Psychology*, 91, 99–124.

Tizard, B., Hughes, M., Carmichael, H. and Pinkerton, G. (1983) Language and social class: is verbal deprivation a myth? *Journal of Child Psychology and Psychiatry and Allied Disciplines*, 24, 533–542.

Toles, T. (1985) Video games and American military ideology. In A. Mosco and R. Wasco (Eds) *Critical Communications Review, 3: Popular Culture and Media Events*. Norwood: Ablex Press.

Tsien, J.Z. (2000) Building a brainier mouse. *Scientific American*, April, 2000.

Vinacke, W.E. (1954) Deceiving experimental subjects. *American Psychologist*, 9, 155.

Vygotsky, L.S. (1962) *Thought and Language*. Cambridge, MA: MIT Press.

Watson, J.B. and Rayner, R. (1920) Conditioned emotional reactions. *Journal of Experimental Psychology*, 3, 1–14.

Weinberg, R.S., Gould, D. and Jackson, A. (1979) Expectations and performance: an empirical test of Bandura's self-efficacy theory. *Journal of Sport Psychology*, 1, 320–331.

Wilson, P.R. (1968) Perceptual distortion of height as a function of ascribed academic status. *Journal of Social Psychology*, 74, 97–102

Woods, B. (1998) *Applying Psychology to Sport.* London: Hodder & Stoughton.

Yerkes, R.M. and Dodson, J.D. (1908) The relationship of strength of stimulus to rapidity of habit formation. *Journal of Comparative Neurology and Psychology*, 18, 459–482.

Zimbardo P.G. (1973) On the ethics of intervention in human psychological research with special reference to the 'Stanford Prison Experiment'. *Cognition* 2(2), 243–255.

Index